Dad,

Remember, Golf is 90% mental, 10% physical. Whenever we play together, I have more fun than anything else in the world. Thanks for the great times we had and the ones to come!

Love, Dawn

Golf
The Greatest Game

USGA Collection

Lake Champlain, New York, circa 1900

GOLF
THE GREATEST GAME

Introduction by John Updike
Reflections on the Game by Arnold Palmer

The USGA Celebrates
Golf in America

HarperCollins*Publishers*

 For information address HarperCollins Publishers, Inc., 10 East 53rd Street, New York, NY 10022. HarperCollins books may be purchased for educational, business, or sales promotional use. For information please write: Special Markets Department, HarperCollins Publishers, Inc., 10 East 53rd Street, New York, NY 10022.

Produced by Jones & Janello, New York
Edited by Amy Janello and Brennon Jones
Executive Editor for the USGA: Pat Ryan
Printed in Italy by Amilcare Pizzi SpA

First Edition

Library of Congress Cataloging-in-Publication Data
Golf—the greatest game/by the United States Golf Association.—1st ed.
p. cm.
Includes index.
ISBN 0-06-017135-9
1. Golf—United States. I. United States Golf Association.
GV981.G67 1994
796.352'0973—dc20 94-8857

94 95 96 97 98/10 9 8 7 6 5 4 3 2 1

Pinehurst Resort and Country Club, North Carolina, 1993. Photo by Seny Norasingh

CONTENTS

Bettmann/UPI

Queens Village, New York, 1930

Preface

Golf is an artist's game, its palette full of dewy grass and azure sky and well-raked bunkers. It is a philosopher's game, engaging wind and water to play strategic tricks on our concentration. And it is a gambler's game, asking us whether it will be the nerve to aim for the flagstick or the caution to settle for a probable bogey.

The game also is about camaraderie, with a weather eye out for thunderheads and a shared contempt for the slower players up ahead. And the endless discussion of whether one piece of equipment is better than another. Back to the locker room, and the conversation turns to mourning for lipped-out putts or misbegotten swing thoughts. Perhaps there is a small exchange of money, but generally not enough to crimp anyone's style.

The founders of the United States Golf Association probably did not express such esoteric thoughts when they came together at a New York club three days before Christmas in 1894. They were trying to determine the best players in the game by holding a national championship. The search they began with that meeting resulted in three championships the first year—the U.S. Amateur, the U.S. Open, and the Women's Amateur. The national championships that followed have provided the world of golf with a century of memorable experiences, exceeding anything the USGA founders could have imagined.

The land they used was open and natural, a cow pasture really. The implements were as fragile as a hickory stick. The greens were slower than today's fairways. Quality control was an unknown phrase in the gutta-percha golf ball factory. The clubhouse was likely to be an old corn crib. The Apple Tree Gang, as the first club came to be known, didn't begin with oak-paneled splendor; the members merely set up a wooden table in an open field from which to dispense libations.

But it was the game itself which mattered—and that is still true. It is the graceful game, the love of outdoor life, the sheer joy of the journey that has bound us together. More than 400,000 of us, at last count, place the bag tag of the United States Golf Association on our equipment. We recognize the value of the game through membership: honorable enough to adhere to the Rules, self-respect enough to call penalties on ourselves, aware enough to insist on sound environmental practices, practical enough to develop new strains of turfgrass, happy enough to pursue the unattainable goal of perfection.

The memories of golf are the stuff of life. If you will indulge me for a moment, I'll tell a story: Once a kidnapper came to my door with a gun, bound my hands and feet behind me, placed tape over my eyes, and shut me in the trunk of his car for most of the next forty-nine hours. My way of fighting the claustrophobia and clinging to sanity for those seemingly endless hours was to replay mentally every golf course I had ever walked, from an unpedigreed municipal course to Augusta National. (Made a lot of birdies, too, and who could deny it?) When my employer had secured my release, one of my first impulses was to go play the courses with real balls and clubs.

Golf grows and grows and grows. Herbert Warren Wind has written that there were fewer than a dozen golfers in the United States in 1888. A century later there were estimates that more than 20 million play golf sporadically, and perhaps 8 million play regularly. More than 14,000 clubs and courses are in operation. Tee times become more precious. The USGA Handicap System has made it possible for the good, the bad, and the ugly golf swings to be matched in a game with a very small wager. Upwards of 5 million fans watch the major championships on television.

But the numbers that interest golfers most are those on the scorecards. It is still a game. Our goal is to create a book that captures the pleasure golf has given over the last hundred years. We have chosen to recall courses full of golfers, sharing the fates of their favorites, win, lose, or draw. We have searched out the average hacker in his habitat, whether that be the public course in his hometown or one of the fabled venues with championship memories.

The United States Golf Association is charged with the responsibility of preserving and protecting the game. Thousands of USGA members help it fulfill this mission. Volunteering vast amounts of time, they see to it that thirteen national championships—for boys and girls, men and women, public links players and mid-amateurs, seniors and international stars—run smoothly. It is our joyful duty to celebrate together the first one hundred years of our history, and it's our pleasure to look forward to another century of the greatest game.

—Reg Murphy
President, United States Golf Association

The Spirit of the Game

John Updike

I NEVER FEEL MORE HAPPILY AMERICAN THAN WHEN ON A GOLF COURSE. GOLF IS a game of space, and America is a spacious land—even more so one hundred years ago when the USGA was founded. Not for the U.S., once the pawky old game took root here, the thrifty Scots' use of waste linksland by the sandy shore. Forests and farms went under to the shoveling crews and horse teams and then the bulldozer and the front loader to make space for the booming drive, the elevated tee, the glimmering water hazard, the cunning dogleg. This largeness of scale, the epic earthworks that carve a winding green firmament beneath the firmament of cloudy blue, is one of the powerful charms that strikes a newcomer to golf, and that continues to entrance the duffer heavy with years. The tennis court is a cage by comparison, and the football field a mirthless gridiron. Only baseball also consecrates a meadow to play, and not one so wide and various, besprinkled with flowers, studded with trees, haunted by wildlife—a giant humming odorous piece of nature. The same course, played ninety times a summer, is never the same; the wind, the wetness of the soil, the thickness and tint of the foliage all affect the flight of the ball and the condition of the lie. Playing golf, we breathe natural vastness, and reclaim Adam's Edenic heritage.

The tools of the game answer to this vastness—the little hard ball, engagingly dimpled all over, and the hawk-faced clubs, with their woolly hoods. When else does a person move an object so far and high with mere musculature, as mystically leveraged by the mechanics of the swing? What a beautiful thing a swing is, what a bottomless source of instruction and chastisement! The average golfer, if I am a fair specimen, is hooked when he hits his first good shot; the ball climbs into the air all of its own, it seems—a soaring speck conjured from the effortless airiness of an accidentally correct swing. And then, he or she, that average golfer, spends endless frustrating afternoons, whole decades of them, trying to recover and tame the delicate wildness of that first sweet swing. Was ever any sporting motion so fraught with difficulty and mystery?

The golf swing is like a suitcase into which we are trying to pack one too many items—if we remember to keep our heads still, we forget to shift our weight; if we remember to shift our weight, we lift our head, or stiffen the left knee, or uncock the wrists too soon. A playing partner of mine has had great luck with the four-part formula "low, slow, inside-out, and finish high." But this is one too many thoughts for me to hold in the perilous two seconds or so between the stately takeaway and the majestic follow-through. The swing thought that worked so well last Wednesday flies out of my head on Sunday. "Arms like ropes," "soft from the top," "turn your back," "hit with your feet," "throw your hands at the hole," "keep the right elbow close to the body," "touch first the left shoulder with your chin and then the right," "think oily"—all have worked for me, if only for a spell. The excitement of hitting the ball and seeing where it will go are too much for me. Of all sports, golf least favors an excitable disposition. You don't have to look as sleepy as Fuzzy Zoeller, or be as expressionless as Davis Love III, but it takes more than a dash of phlegm to apply one's talents steadily over the length of eighteen holes.

This, too, this drawling quality of good golf, seems well suited to our national character. Laconic, cool, easy in the saddle, eyes dryly squinting at the distant horizon—these attributes belong equally to the cowboy and the good golfer. Who is more American, Gary Cooper or Sam Snead? Our champions, from Francis Ouimet to Ben Hogan on up to Fred Couples, tend to be terse types who let the clubs do the talking. Once American golfers, basking in the electronic sunshine that Arnold Palmer turned on, became personable on television and productive of gracious on-the-spot interviews, the underexposed Europeans began to win our championships.

Among the benisons golf bestows upon its devotees is a relative hush. One says "good putt" or "too bad" or "two up and three to go" and there is no obligation to say much more; a worshipful silence attends the long walks between shots, the ignominious searching of the rough, the solemn, squatting appraisal of a treacherous, critical putt. Golf is a constant struggle with one's self, productive of a few grunts and expletives but no extended discourse; it is a mode of meditation, a communion with the laws of aerodynamics, a Puritan exercise in inward exhortation and outward stoicism. Since its rules can be infracted in the privacy of a sand bunker or a sumac grove, it tests the conscience. And it is the only professional game that, under the stress of ever-bigger bucks and crowds, hasn't lost its manners.

How much poorer my sense of my native land would be if I had not, at the age of twenty-five, fallen in love with golf! Many landscapes have been engraved in my consciousness by the pressures of this or that golf shot. The magnificent view, for instance, from the fourth tee of the Cape Ann public course in Essex, Massachusetts—of salt marshes interwoven with arms of steel-blue tidal inlet, cottage-laden peninsulas, and strips of glowing white beach—takes fire in my mind's eye from the exaltation of a well-struck drive drawing into the leftward curve of the fairway, taking a big bound off the slope there, and winding up in fine position to set up a birdie on this scenic patsy of a par five. In Florida, where can one draw close to the original landscape, so thoroughly paved over and air-conditioned, but on a golf course, as one strives to retrieve the ball from the edge of a mangrove swamp or hit it cleanly out of a nest of dried-up palm fronds? The secrets of a locale declare themselves in the interstices of a golf game: the sun-baked spiciness of Caribbean underbrush, the resiny scent and slippery lie beneath a stand of Vermont pines, the numerous anthills of Pennsylvania, like so many cones of spilled coffee grounds. And I am not a golf tourist—the same course day after day holds adventure enough for me, and strangeness, and inexhaustible matter for thought. Until I played golf, for instance, I scarcely knew what grass was—its varying lengths, breadths, resiliencies, and degrees of resistance, gloss, uprightness, and just plain friendliness, as it sits your ball up or snuggles it down, and as it returns your stare as you trudge the length of the long fifteenth fairway to the pot bunker where your errant three-wood, in an ocean of grass, has found a single lonely island of depressed, depressing sand.

People, too, yield up their nuances to golf. As it happened, several of my early, formative playing partners were women: my first wife's aunt, who first put a club into my hand and gave me my first tips (hit the ball with the back of your left hand, she said, and take the putter back as many inches as the putt is feet long); a Japanese widow, somewhat my senior, who told me, after an adequate but unsweet shot, "Not you. Not fly like bird"; an Englishwoman, as smart and spiky as her kiltied shoes, who kept the ball stolidly in the center of the fairway and beat me hollow on her green and soggy layout in suburban London. It was a lesson in feminism to pace the course with these determined females. In the seaside Massachusetts town where I spent my masculine prime, my faithful partners were a local druggist, a pediatrician, and the Baha'i owner of an automatic car wash. Reduced each Wednesday to the same innocence and ineptitude, we loved one another, it seems not too much to say; at least we loved the world we shared for those four hours, a common ground outside of whose bounds we had little to communicate to one another. A priest without his collar, a movie star without his agent, and a Martha's Vineyard hippie without his shoes have been some of my other playing companions, all enjoyable, as the differences between us were quickly subdued to the glories and frustrations of the sport of golf.

No other game, to my knowledge, provides so ready and effective a method of handicapping, which can produce a genuine match between gross unequals. On the ski slopes, the son quickly outspeeds the father; at the backgammon table, the mother consistently outsmarts the daughter; but on the golf course, we play our parents and our children with unfeigned competitive excitement, once the handicap strokes are in place on the card. Golf is a great social bridge, and a great tunnel into the essences of others, for people are naked when they swing—their patience or impatience, their optimism or pessimism, their grace or awkwardness, the very style of their life's desires are all bared. Like children trying to walk and bear cubs trying to climb a tree, they are lovable in their imperfection and then all the more lovable in their occasional triumphs of muscle and will. The putt that wobbles in, the chip that skids up close, the iron that climbs like a rocket and sinks like a plumb line—we cheer such momentary feats as if they were our own. Golf is a competitive experience, yes, but also an aesthetic one—a mutual appreciation that burns away the grit of selfish aggression, or sublimates it, alchemically, into a hovering bonhomie.

On a golf course, I feel free—free of my customary worries, left back at the clubhouse and in the parking lot, and free even of the physical limits placed on my body, as I try to imagine this or that soaring, unerring shot. In Michael Murphy's mystical yet practical *Golf in the Kingdom*, the acolyte–narrator relates of his critical midnight lesson with the guru Shivas Irons: "As I fell into the focus Shivas wanted, my body widened until it embraced the ball all the way to the target. He had said that the club and the ball are one. 'Aye ane fiedle afore ye e'er swung' [all one field before you ever swung] . . . and sure enough I became that field." The spirit of golf is transcendental and free. Americans are not the only people to treasure freedom—all people treasure it, even when they dare not name it—but here above all is freedom proclaimed as a national ideal. After the game's slow start a century ago (our first golf course, St. Andrew's in Yonkers, was founded in 1888, fifteen years after Canadians formed the Montreal Golf Club), the United States took to golf with such a vengeance that, between the Age of Jones and the Age of Nicklaus, it seemed an American game. A curious number of that long era's stars (Byron Nelson, Ben Hogan, Jimmy Demaret, Lee Trevino, Ben Crenshaw) came from Texas, the American superstate, with the widest open spaces and a superabundance of those hot days that bring out golf's subtlest juices. Now, the Europeans are in the game, and not just our old cronies the English and the Scots; even Germany has produced a superstar. In golf, as in every other international activity, the United States must prove itself anew, and this is a good thing. On the first tee, all men, and all nationalities, are equal, and after the eighteenth green, there is no arguing with the scorecard.

Complexity and simplicity: in the tension between them lies the beauty of the real. Golf generates more books, more incidental rules, more niceties of instruction, and more innovations in equipment than any other game, yet it has a scoring system of divine simplicity: as all souls are equal before their Maker, a two-inch putt counts the same as a 250-yard drive. There is a comedy in this, and a certain unfairness even, which make golf an even apter mirror of reality. But its reflection is a kindly one, with some funhouse warps and waves in the glass; it is life without the weight. Or so it has seemed to me, on many a dewy morning and many a long-shadowed afternoon spent in those pretty pieces of America set aside for this grand and gracious form of play.

John Dominis/Life Magazine

Reflections on the Game

Arnold Palmer with Thomas Hauser

Previous spread: A Ben Hogan drive rivets the gallery at the 1952 U.S. Open. Hogan had won the previous two Opens, but this time, at the Northwood Club in Dallas, he would have to settle for third. Julius Boros was champion.

Gracious in defeat, Dick Chapman (above, on right) extends congratulations after George Dunlap's winning putt at the 1931 North and South Championship at Pinehurst No. 2. Note the sand green.

The Bettmann Archive

BACK IN 1975 I WAS FORTUNATE TO BE HONORED AS GOLF'S Man of the Silver Era by a group of writers I'd known and respected for much of my career. It was an emotional moment. And when it came time for me to accept the award, I spoke from the heart.

"I can't tell you how much I appreciate what the game has done for me," I said that night. "I look at the people I've met and the associations I've made through golf. I met my wife, Winnie, through golf. I can't give enough to golf. If I had more, I'd give more. Everything I have I owe to golf. When you honor me, that's a falsehood. You're honoring golf."

Nineteen years have passed since that moment, but my thoughts haven't changed. In fact, if anything, I feel more strongly today than ever about the very special nature of the game. Unlike most major sports in America, it's truly international in scope. And it has a longer tradition of unbroken competition than any other modern sport. I could go back hundreds of years to examine golf's traditions, but two milestones stand out in my mind. One hundred years ago, the United States Golf Association was formed, and since then, the USGA has been the cornerstone of golf here in the United States. On a more personal note, forty years ago, I was fortunate enough to win the USGA Amateur championship. That win marked a turning point in my life. It gave me the confidence I needed to pursue a career in golf, and it has meant more to me over the years than any other victory. "Forty" and "one hundred" are nice round numbers. And every now and then, I like to share my thoughts about golf with people who care. So this seems like a good time to talk about the game I love—a game that is timeless, changeless, and ever-changing.

The most obvious change in golf over recent decades has been its exploding popularity. In 1950 3.2 million Americans played the game. Now the total is 24.8 million, and women are just as enthusiastic as men about the sport. In 1950 there were fewer than 5,000 golf courses in the United States. Now the total is more than 14,000. In 1950 it was said that only rich people played golf, and country-club courses far outnumbered municipal courses.

The Bettmann Archive

Now the United States has some 4,500 more public courses than private ones.

Why has golf been so successful? In my opinion, it's because the game has held on to the traditions that made it great. There's a continuity in golf that one is hard-pressed to find elsewhere in modern America. Look at the ways that golf has remained unchanged.

The natural beauty of golf courses is a good place to start. Being able to play in a beautiful setting is part of the essence of golf. When I'm on a course, I might be in the middle of one of the largest cities in the world with a six-lane superhighway nearby, but I have no sense of that. Instead, I'm in lovely surroundings, and that natural beauty is important to me. Years ago golf courses were beautiful because they were built in stunning locations like Augusta and Pebble Beach. Now spectacular natural settings are hard to find, but course designers work wonders with the resources at their command.

I helped design a course in Florida where, the first time I walked the site, twelve of eighteen holes were under water. Now it's the heart of a thriving residential community, and that's pretty neat. The Palmer Course Design Company planned another course on solid rock on the side of Cheyenne Mountain in Colorado, where the difference in elevation between the high and low holes is four hundred feet. In Taiwan we moved 15 million cubic yards of earth, built a lake, and raised a valley floor three hundred feet to create thirty-six holes. In each case, the result was a course that challenged golfers without sacrificing natural beauty. That's the standard I set for the courses I design for my clients.

And when it comes to my own holdings, I practice what I preach. If you look at Latrobe Country Club in Pennsylvania, you'll see that, since I bought it in 1971, we've landscaped it, and not just with flowers. We put in a full irrigation system so the course would be green everywhere, not just where the old sprinklers reached. In the 1920s and 1930s, my father planted most of the trees that are on the course today. And unless a tree is completely dead, no one is going to cut it down on me. There's a creek that runs through the course, and in the past few years, strip-mine drainage and pollution from a limestone quarry have

Bob Straus

Despite the restrictive Victorian golfwear (top, left), this competitor at the original Baltusrol course gives her drive plenty of zip.

A horseshoe-shaped throng (above) watches Curtis Strange hole out to beat Nick Faldo for the 1988 Open championship at The Country Club in Brookline, Massachusetts.

Recreational golf was in full swing in the 1920s at Hawaii's Mid-Pacific Country Club in the shadow of the Oahu mountains.

tainted the water. It's still usable for irrigation, but it has an ugly look, and I complained to the authorities about it. They're working on it, and I expect that creek will be clean again soon.

In short, over the years, the beauty of golf courses has remained unchanged. Domed stadiums have turned football from a game that was profoundly influenced by nature into one where it can be zero degrees outside and the weather doesn't matter. Baseball has adopted artificial turf, which alters the way the game is played. Boxing paints beer-company logos on its ring canvases. But golf's playing fields are still unspoiled and clean.

The fundamentals of the sport have also remained unchanged. Baseball was once considered *the* traditional American game. But the people who ran our "national pastime" felt the need to jazz up their product. So baseball introduced designated hitters and a new strike zone. One year it told umpires to enforce the balk rule, and a year later it told them to forget about enforcement except when extreme violations occurred. Basketball introduced three-point shots. Tennis now has tiebreaker scoring. Specialization and platooning changed the way football is played.

My view is, "If it isn't broken, don't fix it." And golf isn't broken. I like tradition. I'd hate to see golf do what other sports have done. I don't want the game to change. In fact, I'll go further and say that one very important reason for golf's success over the years is that the basic game hasn't changed.

The only changes golf should encourage are those necessary to preserve the basic game. Let me explain. Golfers today are stronger than they were decades ago, because conditioning techniques are more advanced. Serious golfers practice more than they did when I was young. There have been enormous advances in the technology of the game, because manufacturers now understand the physics of club design and what happens when club meets ball. They're able to redistribute weight with different metals and compounds so that clubs maintain their structural integrity and balance and, at the same time, have a larger "sweet spot" than before. In other words, a golfer today can mishit a ball by a fraction of an inch, and it will stay on the fairway and go almost as far as if it had been hit perfectly. Thirty years ago the same shot might have been short and in the rough.

Also, many of today's golf instructors have gotten so proficient and understand the physics of the game so well that they're able to teach every golfer the fundamentals of a classic swing. When I was young, if a player shot 70 it was, "Hey, leave him alone." Today most players on the Tour work to make their swings technically perfect, because their instructors know how it's done. The benefits of a classic swing can be overrated. I never had one. If I had, would my game have been better? Who knows? Sam Snead and Gene Littler had classic swings. But I can remember when Jack Nicklaus turned pro, some experts said he'd never make it because his elbow moved away from his body on his backswing. And Jack has done reasonably well over the years with his "flying elbow."

John Kelly/The Image Bank

Still, more golfers today than in the past have something close to a classic swing. Pick up a newspaper and you might read that Nick Faldo is going down to see his instructor. Now it's obvious that, after winning two Masters and three British Open championships, Nick Faldo knows how to play golf. But despite his success, he spends several weeks a year with a teacher, working on every nuance of his swing. Where is his thumb positioned on the club? Is he taking his club back too fast? Is the club over an inch too much this way or that?

Yet even though golfers today receive more technical instruction than in the past, par is still par. They play with equipment far superior to what was used decades ago, but improved clubs and balls are still only props for the game. And that's part of the appeal of golf. To counteract advances in technology and instruction, the game has changed to the extent necessary to minimize change. Because so many strong young golfers are hitting the ball farther now than before, old courses have been lengthened where possible and new ones are built longer. In response to innovative clubs that allow more accurate shots, fairways have been narrowed. Today's balls are aerodynamically superior to the ones I used as a boy; but the USGA is constantly on guard to see that manufacturers don't cross over the fine line that protects the integrity of the game and safeguards the challenge of par. And believe me, that's not an easy task.

The mental demands of the sport have also remained unchanged. No matter what anyone does to the clubs, no matter how courses are designed, the need to control your emotions on a golf course is constant. Golf demands total concentration. I can go out and play four brilliant holes, score four birdies in a row. And on the fifth hole, the very same Arnold Palmer using the very same clubs will take a double-bogey. Why? Because I lost my concentration.

Also, more than any other sport, golf requires maturity and judgment. Boris Becker won the most coveted title in tennis, the men's Wimbledon crown, when he was seventeen years old. Tracy Austin was the U.S. Open women's tennis champion at eighteen. Magic Johnson led the Los Angeles Lakers to the NBA championship three years after he graduated from high school.

Escorted by the men in blue, Jack Nicklaus (left) grins at the gallery after his 1980 Open victory at Baltusrol. With that title, Nicklaus joined Willie Anderson, Bobby Jones, and Ben Hogan as four-time Open champions.

Practice, and more practice: 1983 Open champ Jan Stephenson (top, right), who has won sixteen tournaments on the LPGA Tour, follows through on a Florida range.

John Loengard/Life Magazine

Dawn formation for weekenders (above) on the practice green at Mosholu Golf Course, a New York City muni, in 1961.

Jack Botean (right) braves the foul weather at Pelham Country Club in 1961.

Mike Tyson and Muhammad Ali each held boxing's undisputed heavyweight championship at twenty-two. Many Olympic gold-medal winners are in their teens. All of these young men and women are remarkably gifted athletes. But golf has always required far more than physical prowess. There are very few twenty-year-olds who win PGA Tour events. A young golfer might be stronger than an old one and capable of hitting the ball farther, but in golf, the six inches between the ears is the distance that matters most. Likewise, the ability to cope with pressure is more important in golf than in any other sport. You can't swing freely if your muscles are tense. You can't putt if your muscles are tense. Yet when a golfer is under pressure, the tension is there. That never changes.

The passion of golfers for the game has also been constant. Golfers go through stages. When they start, their first goal might be to break 100, and they'll work like a dog to get there. Then they do it; it's a tremendous achievement. And the next thing you hear is, "I want to break 90." That might take years. They take lessons; they practice. The day they break 90 it's as though they've reached heaven. After that, it's 80. And they have to work very hard to break 80. A golfer might get to 82 or 83 and grow fearful that his tombstone will read, "He couldn't break 80." But whether a golfer is playing poorly or well, whether he's shooting 99 or 70, if he takes the game seriously the challenge is always there. A golfer can't dictate what his opponents shoot. He can't wave his arms or tackle a fellow competitor who's getting ready to putt. But he can always reach within himself to bring out the best in his battle against the laws of physics and par.

I've heard it said that golfers on the pro tour today don't

John Loengard/Life Magazine

Babe Zaharias lets one fly at the 1946 Women's Amateur at Southern Hills Country Club in Tulsa; she went on to win.

Cornell Capa/Life Magazine

excite galleries the way we did thirty years ago. I guess one reason is that so many good golfers are out there now that no one player can win enough tournaments to become dominant. In my younger days there were a handful of top contenders. People could pick a favorite, and as often as not, one of us would win. That meant we were able to attract the attention necessary for fans to get to know us and build a following. Take The Masters as an example. In recent years, The Masters has been won by Larry Mize, Sandy Lyle, Nick Faldo (twice), Ian Woosnam, Fred Couples, Bernhard Langer, and José Maria Olazabal. Compare that with the first seven years of the 1960s, when Jack Nicklaus, Gary Player, and I won seven out of seven Masters titles.

I personally think that someone will come along in the next decade and start winning tournaments in bunches the way a few of us did thirty years ago. That's the nature of competitive sports. Every now and then an athlete who's simply better than the rest arrives on the scene. Take basketball as an example. Wilt Chamberlain led the NBA in scoring for seven years in a row, and during his career scored 8,000 more points than anyone who played before him. A lot of people thought those records would never be broken. Then Kareem Abdul-Jabbar scored 6,968 more points than Wilt. And in an era when the level of competition in the NBA was higher than ever, Michael Jordan won seven consecutive scoring titles.

But getting back to golf, my view is that winning and stirring passions have a lot to do with attitude. And that's one area where golf—at least golf on the Tour—has changed. In 1954, the year I turned pro, the total prize money on the PGA Tour for the entire year was $600,819. I had to win to make a good living. Now, fast forward to 1993. In a single year Nick Price won $1,478,557. Twenty-six golfers had more than $600,000 in official Tour earnings. In fact, one player won $982,875 in 1993 without winning a single tournament.

I've said many times that I'd rather win one tournament in my entire life than make the cut every week, and I still feel that way. I haven't won in a while, but I'm still trying. And believe me, I'm still out there to win, not just to make a "good" showing. But sometimes I think, with all the money at stake, there are guys on the Tour today who play it safe rather than go for the win. They're content to finish eighth or ninth, pick up their paychecks, and move on to the next tournament. These are very skilled golfers, and most of them are very nice men. But the money has taken away their hunger, and they aren't following the road that leads to becoming a hero.

So golf to me is the physical act of playing; it involves the mental challenge of playing. But more important than any of the things I've talked about so far, it's the moral code of the game. That moral code embodies the spirit of golf. It's at the heart of our tradition. It hasn't changed over the years. And it's what separates golf from all other sports.

Golfers are on the honor system: We play by the Rules,

With part of the gallery at ground level, Jug McSpaden coaxes home the winning putt at Tam O'Shanter in the 1943 All-American Open.

Next spread: Those who wanted the best views of Ben Hogan and Sam Snead at the 1956 Canada Cup in Wentworth, England, run for it. The Americans won the title.

Bettmann/UPI

and we enforce them against ourselves. That's the essence of our sport, and every serious golfer knows it. Overall, the moral standards of society have declined in recent years, but the morality of golf hasn't changed. Some people say that's because golf attracts people of high integrity to begin with. Maybe it does, but I think it's more a case of the game and the people who play it demanding integrity from all who participate. We won't tolerate anything less. The game generates respect, and those of us who play it take pride in enforcing the Rules ourselves. I can't imagine a major league baseball player telling the umpire, "You missed the call; he tagged me; I was out." Or an NFL running back saying, "There's no touchdown; I stepped out of bounds." But golfers at every level of the game do that all the time. We even monitor our own equipment and call penalties on ourselves if we discover an extra club in our golf bag.

I remember one incident when Jay Hebert was in the woods. No one but his caddie was with him. Jay came out and said, "Add a stroke; my ball moved." Jay's caddie hadn't seen the ball move, but Jay had, and that was the end of it. Even though thousands of dollars were involved, the integrity of the game was paramount in Jay's mind. And as a golfer, I like the fact that I'm playing with people who feel the same way about the Rules as I do. All true golfers pride themselves on their integrity.

The etiquette of golf, with its emphasis on good manners, has also remained unchanged. Like golf, tennis was once considered a "gentleman's" sport, with roots in the upper class. And like golf, tennis has spread dramatically to the masses. But players in today's showcase tennis tournaments often throw their rackets, berate linesmen, and make obscene gestures to fans. And all that happens is the umpire says, "Keep playing." Basketball players trash-talk. Hockey players fight with regularity. Other sports condone this type of behavior because they think it broadens their fan base. And sure, maybe if Greg Norman and Curtis Strange got into a fistfight on the final hole of the U.S. Open, more people would turn on the television the next time they were paired together. But it wouldn't be golf. And I have to feel that the public appreciates the etiquette of golf, because spectators who pay $30 to attend a tournament understand that their ticket doesn't give them the right to boo and jeer. And although people look at other professional athletes and say they've become spoiled and make far too much money, I rarely hear that complaint about professional golfers.

I get upset when someone doesn't behave properly on a golf course. And that's true whether the offender is a touring pro at a major tournament or a fourteen-year-old playing on a municipal course. Respect for the codes of conduct of the game goes to the heart of golf. And in that regard, there's no doubt in my mind that the USGA has been a special blessing. From time to time someone suggests that the touring pros should make their own rules or do this or do that separate from the USGA. But I think that would be a disaster. The presence and authority of the

FPG

Even in defeat, Walter Hagen (above, seated) was unruffled. George Duncan was too good for Hagen in this exhibition match in Britain in the early 1920s.

At the 1937 Masters (top, right): Byron Nelson looked like an also-ran—until he made up six strokes on leader Ralph Guldahl (on right) on the twelfth and thirteenth and went on to win.

Culver Pictures

Bettmann/UPI

USGA reinforces adherence to the Rules and the etiquette of golf at all levels of the game.

Indeed, part of the very special nature of golf is that total strangers of vastly different ability and background can meet on a golf course and play competitively thanks to the Rules of play, equipment standards, and handicapping procedures established by the USGA. I can go to a golf course in a city I've never been to before and meet a corporate executive from New York or a truckdriver from Dallas, and we can enjoy the competitive camaraderie of a round of golf. I can't go out and play basketball competitively with Shaquille O'Neal or football with Joe Montana or tennis with Jim Courier. And if I were thirty years old again, I still couldn't; there's no way to level those playing fields. But anyone can play golf with me. And in the end, that's the true magic of the game. What it means to the everyday golfer.

Golf is fun, and it brings out the best in people. When you take a club and swing it perfectly, and your hands finish high where they're supposed to be, your body has completed a wonderful harmonic motion, and there's a tremendous sense of physical achievement. You don't have to see the ball to know you've hit a good shot. When you play by the Rules, defy mental demons, overcome every challenge, and enjoy a walk in the country at the same time—that's being alive.

When I was younger, I used to walk down a fairway and say to myself, "This is the same fairway Bobby Jones walked down" or, "This is the hole where Gene Sarazen scored his famous double-eagle." Now when I'm on the course, I'm more inclined to reminisce about my own experiences. But beyond that, for me golf hasn't really changed. I still have a special feeling for the game's history and traditions. My greatest respect is reserved for men like Byron Nelson and Walter Hagen, who not only were great players but also gave everything that was in them back to the game. And I like to think that the next time the U.S. Open is at Cherry Hills, some young golfer will tee up on the first hole and say to himself, "This is where Arnold Palmer drove the green that day in 1960 when he shot his final-round 65."

My love for golf is enduring and unchanged.

One Hundred Years of the USGA

John Strawn

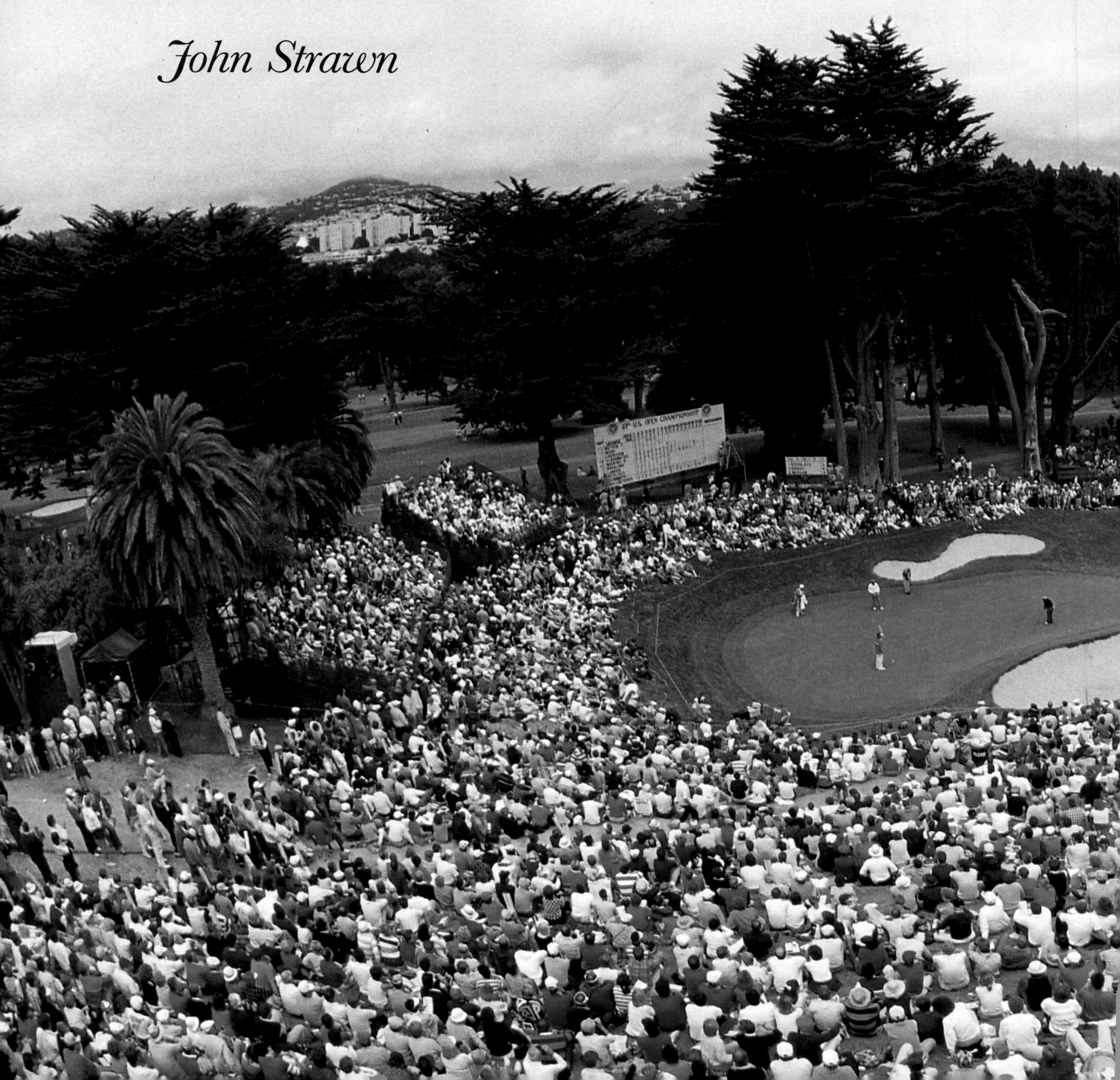

Focus on Sports

Previous spread: The final-day gallery gathers around the eighteenth at San Francisco's Olympic Club to watch Scott Simpson run in the last putt to beat Tom Watson by one stroke at the 1987 Open.

Five aspirants at the unofficial 1894 Amateur (above): Louis Biddle prepares to play as (from left) James Parks, Laurence Curtis, C. B. Macdonald, and George Armstrong wait their turn, at St. Andrew's in Yonkers, New York.

The Bettmann Archive

CHARLIE MACDONALD WAS A STUBBORN MAN, AND IN the infancy of American golf, when not merely the best players but every golfer in the United States could have gathered in a single smoking car, Macdonald was eager to affirm his reputation as the country's finest golfer. His chance finally came in the fall of 1894, and it was out of his fury at failing to win—a failure he blamed on irregular conditions and arbitrary rulings—that the United States Golf Association was born.

Macdonald had learned the game at its fountainhead, on the Old Course at St. Andrews. Though only sixteen, he had traveled from his Chicago home to his father's native Scotland in 1872 to "complete my education at the university." The summer before Charlie matriculated, his grandfather, a resident of St. Andrews and a member of the Royal & Ancient Golf Club, bought him several clubs crafted at Old Tom Morris's shop and set the boy loose on the links. His initial impression was that golf was "a silly game for old men," as he recalled in his 1928 memoir, *Scotland's Gift—Golf.* But, given that there was "nothing to do in St. Andrews but play golf and bathe," he acquired the game's skills quickly. In foursomes with local artisans and lairds, among resident scholars and celebrated summer visitors like Anthony Trollope and John Stuart Mill—come to savor St. Andrews' long, soft summer days—Macdonald ultimately surrendered to golf's charms.

Playing with Old Tom and his brilliant son, Young Tom—winner of the Open championship thrice in succession and triumphant once again the year Macdonald arrived in Scotland—Charlie mastered the robust, rocking swing suited to St. Andrews' blustery winds. He foreswore Old Tom's habit of bathing every morning in the frigid waters of St. Andrews' East Bay, but the force of the old man's rectitude, his golfing *righteousness*, saturated Charlie's soul like the chill of a corrosive *haar*, the piercing fog that stalks the links from the North Sea.

"Golf was so simple at St. Andrews," Macdonald recalled. The plain pieties of Scottish golf, its guilelessness, captivated Macdonald, who could chant the golfer's litany with a convert's

USGA Collection

zeal: Play the ball as it lies. Don't touch the ball with anything but a club until it's holed out. *Abide by the spirit of the game.*

Macdonald returned in 1874 not just to a golfless Chicago, but to a United States with no golf courses at all, an Edmund Hillary languishing on the plains. On business trips to Britain Macdonald played, but he was unable to stir up any interest in golf among his friends in the Midwest until 1893, when a group of English golfers working at the Chicago World's Fair talked up the game. That year Macdonald and his friends built the first eighteen-hole golf course in the United States, the Chicago Golf Club. (The handful of courses that had recently sprung up on the East Coast were all nine holes or fewer.) The course Macdonald designed veered right in a gentle arc, perfectly accommodating his natural slice.

In the meantime, a group of New Yorkers led by a transplanted Scot named John Reid founded in 1888 what is today the oldest continuously existing golf club in the United States, St. Andrew's, playing first on a three-hole course, then a six-hole course, then briefly on yet another six-hole layout rambling through an old apple orchard in Yonkers. The gentlemen of the American St. Andrew's—women were excluded from their company—were thereafter known as The Apple Tree Gang, and Reid, Macdonald's senior by a generation, was lionized as "the father of American golf." But Macdonald was its godfather, and with his missionary certainty, his proselyte's fervor, he compelled

With his sons caddying, John Reid (above, on right) and friends gather on a green at what would become his St. Andrew's Golf Club.

Four-time British Open champion Old Tom Morris (below), a famous resident at Scotland's St. Andrews, played into his eighties.

With the 1933 British Open within his grasp, Denny Shute (right) watches Craig Wood putt out on the eighteenth at St. Andrews Old Course.

Bettmann/UPI

FPG

Robert Todd Lincoln (above), son of the sixteenth U.S. president, demonstrates his turn-of-the-century form off the first tee at Chicago Golf Club.

The USGA Executive Committee at Chicago Golf Club in 1912 (top, right): from left, vice-president J. S. Clark, president Silas H. Strawn, committeeman James L. Taylor, treasurer William F. Morgan, and committeeman Frank L. Woodward.

Courtesy Chicago Golf Club

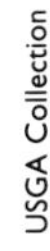

every golfer and club in America to heed his St. Andrean convictions about golf's proper playing. The United States Golf Association owes its existence to Charlie Macdonald's fury at finding his golf ball nestled against a stone wall after a "foozle"—a topped shot—on the day he expected finally to confirm his exalted reputation.

Macdonald's mishap occurred in September 1894 at Newport, Rhode Island, Golf Club, presided over by Theodore Havemeyer of the sugar trust. Macdonald and nineteen fellow competitors had gathered there for what was advertised as the first American golf championship—two days of medal play, eighteen holes each day over Newport's nine-hole course. Assessed two penalty strokes for the ball he struck against the stone wall, Macdonald lost the medal by one stroke. In the words of Herbert Warren Wind, "Charlie Macdonald took the defeat hard." It was not merely that a real golf course would not have stone dikes bisecting its fairways, Macdonald protested, but that amateur championships in Great Britain were exclusively match-play tournaments.

The St. Andrew's club had scheduled just such a match-play event that October. Macdonald won his first day's matches easily, then went to a dinner party given by the architect Stanford White and stayed up until five o'clock in the morning. A bit shaky at breakfast, he followed White's suggestion to take strychnine pellets to perk himself up before setting out for his morning match. The remedy worked well enough for Macdonald to play himself into the finals, but the steak and champagne White decreed for lunch bred "wretched golf that afternoon," and Macdonald was runner-up again, as he had been at Newport. Well, so what? Macdonald argued. With no national golfing association to organize and sanction a championship, how could there be a national champion? The St. Andrew's match-play championship was utterly ersatz. What was needed was an organization whose members were disinterested and above the fray, detached from commerce and ruled only by love of the game, to authorize an authentic national championship.

Three days before Christmas in 1894, heeding Macdonald's complaints, Henry Tallmadge hosted a dinner party at the Calumet Club in New York, at the northeast corner of Fifth Avenue and Twenty-ninth Street. Havemeyer of the Newport Golf Club was there, and Reid of St. Andrew's, and Laurence Curtis and P. S. Sears of The Country Club in Brookline, Massachusetts, and Samuel Parrish and General J. H. Barber of Shinnecock Hills on Long Island, the finest of the East Coast's new courses. And from the west came Arthur Ryerson and Charlie Macdonald of Chicago Golf Club.

Over claret and through a pall of cigar smoke, one assumes, Havemeyer moved "that the Amateur Golf Association of the United States be, and hereby is formed . . . ." The motion carried unanimously, according to the minutes preserved at Golf House, the USGA's headquarters in Far Hills, New Jersey. The Amateur Golf Association soon changed its name to the United States Golf Association, reflecting its willingness to sanction an Open championship, which would inevitably involve professional players. Havemeyer was chosen as the organization's first president, and then—no surprise—Charlie Macdonald took the floor to move the adoption of the association's five "objects," or goals.

The first, predictably, was "to promote the interests of the game of golf." The second was "to establish and enforce

USGA Collection

Henry O. Tallmadge (above) hosted the dinner at which the USGA was formed—and served as its first secretary.

Members of Shinnecock Hills Golf Club (below) take the sun on the porch of their handsome new clubhouse, designed by Stanford White.

Spectators (right) at Meadow Brook Men's Club in 1896 follow—at a distance—a match in progress.

Courtesy Shinnecock Hills Golf Club

USGA Collection

uniformity of the Rules of the game," while the third made the USGA's Executive Committee the "final authority in matters of controversy," of which there would be plenty. The USGA also expected to establish "as far as possible a uniform system of handicapping," a job it has struggled with now for a century, sifting through mountains of sand. Its final task was to decide where its two national championships—the Amateur and the Open—would be held. Thus, with grand aims and a charming simplicity, and fueled by Charlie Macdonald's indignation, the USGA was launched.

I DWELL ON THE USGA'S YOUTH NOT OUT OF AN ANTIQUARIAN interest, but because I think the USGA's personality was formed when its bright-eyed ideals congealed in an inherently conservative organizational structure. There has always been continuity on the USGA's Executive Committee, and the current members serve with the man who served with the man . . . who parleyed with Charlie Macdonald. Only now that man might be a woman. Had the bylaws provided for the periodic election of an entirely new slate of members, rather than for a steady but modest turnover, the USGA would not be what it is. The USGA has changed along with the game, but the ancient spirit persists.

In *its* first one hundred years, the United States had spread across a territory so extensive Thomas Jefferson thought it would

Bettmann/UPI

USGA Collection

Walter Hagen's second and last Open victory, in 1919 at Brae Burn Country Club in Massachusetts (left), was sealed by a stroke with this putt in a playoff.

The First Ladies of the land, Mrs. Harding (above, on right) and Mrs. Coolidge, cheer golfers at the 1921 Open at Columbia Country Club in Chevy Chase, Maryland.

absorb a thousand generations. The historian Frederick Jackson Turner, a contemporary of Charlie Macdonald's, argued in a famous essay that the supply of cheap public land, the social safety valve of America's celebrated western frontier, had dried up by the end of the nineteenth century—at, coincidentally, almost exactly the moment the USGA was formed. More people now lived in cities than on farms, and the public health was threatened by fouled air—from coal smoke, not cars—and crowded living. Parks were seen as an antidote to the stifling conditions of city life; golf courses, blending the benefits of a rural excursion with the safety and control of a well-managed landscape, were specialized parks. And if Turner's thesis was correct, they would have a plentiful supply of caddies.

The USGA was an instrument in borrowing the great Scottish pastime and making it America's own. Henry James, an emigré to the Old World, regarded the country club as America's only contribution to civilization. The country club meant power, and status, and finally it meant golf. No matter how carefully its players adhered to the rules and spirit of the game Charlie Macdonald loved, golf was transformed in America by its social settings, by the great economic power of the United States and the creative energies of its people. Americans built courses on land the Scots would have left for the woodsman. Americans grew better grass and irrigated the turf to make fairways green in drought and heat. The USGA, through its Green Section, was a pioneer in supporting the study of turfgrasses, and because its work was so successful, American golfers came to expect perfect lies.

NOT LONG AFTER THE USGA WAS FOUNDED, AN AMERICAN named Coburn Haskell—a friend of Charlie Macdonald, no less—invented the rubber-cored ball, as great a technological leap as the gutta-percha had been over the feathery. The Haskell

USGA Collection

ball inspired the first lament that equipment was ruining the game, a cry that echoes through the annals of the USGA like the wail of a murdered ancestor. Before it was even a decade old, the USGA was toiling to defend its members' poor, beleaguered golf courses from the power of innovation, against more resilient balls and novel clubs. Banning the pool cue one player hoped to putt with in the first Amateur was easy, but what about scored faces on irons, concave-faced clubs, or a center-shafted putter? In 1897 the USGA considered a par-four hole as one of more than 165 yards but fewer than 310. By 1911 the par four's length had been extended to between 226 and 425 yards. The present scale, adopted in 1956, has endured for nearly four decades because the USGA, having previously determined a golf ball's minimum size and weight, in 1976 imposed an overall distance limit on the ball.

Haskell had offered Macdonald an interest in his rubber-cored-ball company, but Macdonald told him, "I have made it a principle never to receive any profit . . . from my association with the game of golf. She is a mistress whom I adore, and I can do nothing that would taint the relationship with commercialism." Macdonald, a businessman himself, had no objection to Haskell's making money with his new golf ball, but for a USGA committee-

When the competition is over, no matter what the stakes, the bonhomie comes naturally: Bobby Jones (above, on right) relaxes with Jock Hutchison (center) and Tom Kerrigan; (top, right) a disappointed Arnold Palmer congratulates Jack Nicklaus after his 1962 Open playoff win; and (bottom, right) club golfers at Cherry Hills in Colorado call it a day.

Courtesy Oakmont Country Club

John Dominis/Life Magazine

man to have done so would have been unconscionable. Would there not be the temptation to urge the adoption of the patented Haskell as a standard ball? The strict ethic of the USGA forbade such conflicts of interest, and not just for members of the USGA Executive Committee.

Anyone older than fifteen who caddied, for example, was barred from amateur competition by the USGA's first codification of amateur status, along with golf-course architects, sporting-goods salesmen, and greenkeepers. These strictures were relaxed over the years and seem niggling today. In 1926 the USGA ruled that Philip Turnesa, member of the famous family of golfing brothers, enjoyed "unusual opportunities to practice" because he was working for his father as an assistant greenkeeper. Therefore, he could "no longer continue in his position and retain his amateur status."

In his annual address an early USGA president railed, too, against "clubs which are not germane to the spirit of this organization—clubs which are gotten up for the purpose of making money, [for] booming worthless real estate, or it may be hotels. . . . I strongly feel that this Association cannot take too high ground in treating with such clubs." Golf, he concluded, was a *gentleman's* game—golf's grand illusion. What he meant to emphasize, of course, were sportsmanship, honest conduct, and fair play, qualities he thought exclusive to men of his race and class.

American golf was not, in its early days, the game of the people Macdonald had learned in Scotland, where plasterers played with rectors and carpenters with deans. American golf was a game of bluebloods—and mostly male at that. However, women were attracted to the game, and their own Amateur championship was first held in 1895. British clubs—even the R&A—tended to play over public links, but until the past few decades, golf in America was yoked to the private country club, and its championships are still held largely on these venerable member courses. Public golf has a long history in the United States—the first public course, Van Cortlandt Park in the Bronx, New York, is almost as old as the United States Golf Association. But though public clubs could and did join the USGA, their players did not participate in its governance, and the popular image of golf as a pastime of the wealthy persisted. The USGA created an Amateur Public Links championship in 1922, and now more than half its member clubs are associated with public courses. Some cynics suggested that the Public Links tournament was a way of keeping "them," meaning the public course golfer, out of "our" Amateur championship. But, whether at country club or muni, all real golf in America was played, as the golf card said, "under USGA Rules."

THE USGA'S HISTORY INEVITABLY REFLECTS THE COUNTRY'S social evolution. When segregation governed American race relations, the USGA accommodated itself to its member clubs' restricted practices, and it long honored a gentleman's

Lee Elder (above) breaks the color barrier at the 1975 Masters.

Judy Bell (top, right) of Colorado, a talented amateur player, became in 1987 the first woman elected to the USGA Executive Committee.

Leonard Kamsler

Robert Walker

agreement. But the USGA never formally adopted a racially exclusive policy, as the PGA had done in limiting its membership to professional golfers of the "Caucasian race." At the U.S. Open at Shinnecock Hills in 1896, both John Shippen, an African-American whose father was a minister to the Shinnecock Indians, and Oscar Bunn, a member of the Shinnecock tribe, played, over the objections of at least some of the golf professionals, most of whom were transplanted Scotsmen. USGA president Theodore Havemeyer didn't blink. "We will play the Open with you," he said to the grumbling professionals, "or without you." Shippen, who finished fifth among twenty-eight competitors, would play in five more U.S. Opens, the last in 1913, and is celebrated today as the first native-born American professional golfer.

In 1938, however, the USGA refused to accept an Open entry from an African-American golfer. And when the Miami Country Club notified the USGA "that it would not permit Negroes to compete in the 1952 Amateur Public Links championship on its course," the USGA, reluctant to intrude on what it regarded as the prerogative of a member club, acquiesced. But the USGA moved in cautious conformity with America's cultural shift, and in 1959 William Wright won the Public Links in Denver, the first African-American to win a USGA championship. In 1987, Judy Bell, a longtime USGA volunteer and amateur player from Colorado, took her seat as the first woman elected to the USGA's Executive Committee. Five years later John Merchant, a Connecticut lawyer and the first African-American graduate of the University of Virginia Law School, joined the Executive Committee, the same year that Leroy Richie, an African-American lawyer, was appointed the USGA's general counsel.

THE USGA IS AN ALMOST EXACT CONTEMPORARY OF THE modern Olympic Games, the only organization in sports that ever had anything like the USGA's obsession with preserving unsullied amateurism. The committee members of the USGA have always been volunteers serving without compensation. Golf is the only sport whose welfare is overseen and whose Rules are

USGA Collection

set by amateurs. Today the Executive Committee's work is supported by a large staff, but its mission remains the one conceived at the Calumet Club in 1894—tending to the good of the game. As in all matters of value, there have been disagreements over what constitutes the good, but the weight of the USGA's traditions has effectively held conflicts of interest at bay.

The USGA intended from its inception to play according to the Rules prescribed by the R&A, but then straightaway opened a tiny breach when Macdonald, as the first chairman of the committee on Rules, suggested just a couple of little changes to make golf "more adaptable to American links." The USGA would part company with the R&A over the out-of-bounds rule, over the penalty for an unplayable lie, over the center-shafted putter—the USGA condoned it, the R&A banned it—and over the legality of steel-shafted clubs. Arguing that "it conferred no playing advantage" and "would conserve the supply of hickory to an important extent"—for what purpose, heaven knows—the USGA permitted the steel shaft in 1925. The R&A followed its lead three years later. Golf's two governing bodies sometimes drifted apart, like figures in a dance, moving with different steps to the same music, but seemed always to embrace at the end of the

USGA Collection

USGA Collection

An unofficial U.S. women's golf team (top, left), formed by Glenna Collett (sixth from right), arrives in Southampton in 1930. Its matches against the British women would prove to be the precursor of the Curtis Cup, first held in 1932.

In 1920 the USGA Executive Committee (bottom, left), visits Britain to consult with the R&A on the Rules.

During the final of the 1963 Amateur, R. H. Sikes (above) seeks relief from what he believes is a hole made by a burrowing animal. Officials Frank Hannigan (standing) and Joseph C. Dey deny his plea; Sikes would eventually lose to Deane Beman.

evening. After fifty years of *ad hoc* accommodations, the USGA and the R&A established their joint authority at a summit conference in 1951, agreeing to periodic mutual review. The world now plays golf by the same set of Rules.

IN 1901 USGA PRESIDENT R. H. ROBERTSON OF SHINNECOCK Hills Golf Club, addressing the delegates gathered at the annual meeting at Delmonico's in New York City, said, "Nothing can come to America and stay very long without being Americanized in character; and I hope this game will be no exception to this rule. I should like to see American golf." Robertson's comments made Macdonald apoplectic—"The troubles," he wrote, "began right here"—but Robertson simply spoke the truth about what was happening to golf in the United States. Just as American culture was being enriched by the traditions of its new citizens, then passing by the millions through Ellis Island, America's sporting culture was learning new attitudes from golf. In the cauldron of American culture, golf was transfigured and, with it, perforce, the Rules.

Americans have always preferred four-balls to foursomes, stroke play to match. A bent for keeping an individual score for every round has traditionally distinguished American from Scottish golfers. Americans loved to measure themselves, to know where they stood, because the social structure they inhabited was fluid, its distinctions rarely fixed. Americans hated the stymie, too, because it affronted their sense of justice. Americans, an Englishman observed, play golf "with pain that is almost pleasure."

The stymie was the closest thing golf ever had to a goalie. In match play, a player could "lay a stymie" by stopping his ball between his opponent's ball and the cup. The Western Golf Association, soon joined by other sectional organizations, stopped playing the stymie in 1917, standing against the USGA's authority. Nothing in golf was more controversial. The debate raged for three decades, in the golf press and at the annual meetings of the USGA. The stymie was finally abolished at the great Rules summit between the USGA and the R&A, effective in 1952.

The English language preserves the word, but the stymie is gone from golf. Once the stymie was abolished, there were two games of golf: the shots from tee to green and the putting game. American golf forced this transformation, and now we routinely mark and clean our balls on the green, scarcely comprehending what an abominable act this would have seemed fifty years ago. Players mark and clean even at St. Andrews. (And, as further evidence of the influence of American golf, the Old Course has irrigated its fairways.) As Joseph Dey, the USGA's executive secretary who shepherded American golf into the modern age, said, the rule against the stymie "was made by the people—which is the best kind of law, because an unpopular law is generally unenforceable and so pointless to have on the books."

Hometown heroes (above): 1925 Amateur champion Bobby Jones, runner-up Watts Gunn, and Jones biographer O.B. Keeler.

Judy Oliver, now on the USGA Women's Committee, is a three-time Curtis Cup team member (top, right).

The Bettmann Archive

John Kelly

THE AMATEUR WAS *THE* CHAMPIONSHIP THROUGH THE FIRST third of the USGA's history—of the four major championships in Bobby Jones's grand slam in 1930, two were amateur titles—but the best playing inevitably shifted toward the professionals. Ultimately the U.S. Open, as the greatest challenge in golf, would outstrip the Amateur in prestige. The Open was last won by an amateur in 1933, and the next year the USGA hired Dey as its executive secretary—later director—dual milestones marking the end of American golf's travels through childhood. Dey manned the bridge as the USGA negotiated its modus vivendi with the R&A and accommodated itself to the ascendancy of professional golf. A former sportswriter who also penned forgettable short fiction under the nom de plume Howard Holt, Dey became the USGA's leading expert on Rules. The organization he joined in 1934 had never sold broadcast rights to any of its championships, but by the time Dey left the USGA to head the PGA Tour in 1969, the USGA's revenues from telecasts of the U.S. Open had given it financial muscle, funds to support an expanded program of turf research, to scrutinize and test equipment, and to devote the same attention to the championships that didn't bring in money as to the U.S. Opens. There are now thirteen USGA championships—not just the Opens and Amateurs, but Senior Opens and Amateurs, Junior championships for boys and girls, and the Mid-Amateurs. The creation of the Mid-Amateur championship marked the reluctant recognition that in tolerating golf scholarships for college players, the USGA had effectively turned over the Amateur to what Frank Hannigan called the "pre-professionals," and needed an event to test the skills of slightly more mature players. Many reinstated professionals play in the Mid-Amateur, and the USGA has long been generous in its willingness to restore players to amateur status.

Professional domination of the U.S. Opens—a Women's Open was started in 1953—bolstered the USGA's determination to maintain its strict Rules on amateurism. Men and women who made their living from golf had an advantage over players for whom golf was a hobby. But in what, exactly, did making a living at golf consist? Here the USGA committeemen struggled endlessly to make clear distinctions. When Frank Hannigan—who would later serve as the USGA's executive director and, like Dey and his successor, P. J. Boatwright, earn acclaim for his expertise on Rules—drafted a white paper on the evolution of the USGA's view of amateur status, it was forty single-spaced pages long. The great breach in what Hannigan called this "awful realm" was the USGA's decision to allow college golfers to accept scholarships without compromising their amateur status. But long before casting that blind eye, the USGA had bumped up against the wall of its own certainties, and never more so than in the aftermath of its troubled decision to exile Francis Ouimet.

When it banned Ouimet from amateur competition in 1917, because he had an interest in a sporting-goods company, the USGA learned just how fiercely the golfing public embraced its heroes. Ouimet was not just any golfer. In 1913, as a twenty-year-old playing at The Country Club in Massachusetts, where he had once caddied, Ouimet won the U.S. Open over the great British professionals Harry Vardon and Ted Ray.

The year before, the USGA had designated those eligible for the Amateur by publishing its first handicap list, naming all the 450 or so golfers in the country with a handicap of six or lower. Ouimet was then playing off three. By 1914 he was at scratch, a more suitable stature for the U.S. Open champion—it is hard to imagine someone with a three handicap winning the Open.

Ouimet's determination to play as an amateur was unusual. The great professionals of his era, like Walter Hagen and Gene Sarazen, and their younger successors, like Ben Hogan and Byron Nelson, Sam Snead and Jimmy Demaret, were drawn from the caddie ranks. Before the rise of college golf, caddying and professional golf were inextricably linked, with caddies lured by the purses on the PGA Tour—so much so that when golf carts came on the scene in the 1950s, the PGA abhorred their use, sure that the pool from which professional golfers were drawn would dry up. The early professionals learned to shave hickory shafts and repair broken clubs, and their lives were financially insecure.

The first Open, an afterthought to the first official Amateur championship in 1895, was a thirty-six-hole tournament played on the day after the real championship's final match. The winner pocketed $150 and a gold medal. It was not until the 1920 Open at Inverness Club in Toledo, Ohio, that professionals were granted the privileges of the clubhouse. Bobby Jones, a Harvard-educated lawyer, was the age's quintessential amateur—not simply because he was an incomparable player, but because he refused, in the spirit of Charlie Macdonald, to commercialize his success. Jones was revered by the USGA, and never more so than when he turned down the gift of a house from his friends in Atlanta—an act the USGA president called "a magnificent thing," because accepting it would not have violated any USGA stricture. Ouimet was similarly imbued with the spirit of amateurism.

Hy Peskin/Life Magazine

The one-iron. Ben Hogan approaches the eighteenth green at Merion in the last round of the 1950 Open. This shot, and his subsequent two-putt for par, would put him into a playoff, which he would win with a fine 69.

The Bettmann Archive

Bettmann/UPI

The Bettmann Archive

Walking into history—twenty-year-old Francis Ouimet and ten-year-old caddie Eddie Lowery (far left), en route to Ouimet's stunning victory at the 1913 Open at The Country Club.

Byron Nelson (above) was such a popular figure at the Tam O'Shanter All-American in 1944 that he couldn't even quench his thirst without the adoring gaze of fans and caddies.

Gene Sarazen (left) started golf as a caddie. In 1922, at Skokie Country Club in Illinois, he became Open champion, to the delight of his caddie.

USGA Rules official Harry Easterly (above) makes sure Brian Claar, Bill Britton, and Kirk Triplett keep up the pace at the 1993 Open at Baltusrol.

Grant Spaeth (top, right), serving the double role of USGA president and Rules official at the 1990 Open at Medinah, keeps pace with competitor Jeff Sluman.

Amy Janello

Robert Walker

The USGA's decision to declare Ouimet a professional was greeted with hostility, especially among western golfers, for whom the magazine *Golf* spoke. It referred to the "Ouimet outrage," labeled the USGA the "five per-cent corporation," and denounced it as unrepresentative and a "disintegrating force in golf." These were the same contentious westerners who were abandoning the stymie.

In 1918 Ouimet was inducted into the Army, giving the USGA a way to reinstate him without admitting any wrong in having banned him in the first place. The dispute died with a whimper, and not even the western golfers could sustain their outrage in the golf boom of the twenties. Ouimet, who won his first Amateur in 1914, the year following his Open victory, and his second in 1931, served for years on the USGA's Executive Committee and in 1951 would drive himself in as the first American captain of the R&A. In no player were the USGA's ideals more firmly fixed.

THE OUIMET CASE HELPED THE USGA EARN A REPUTATION for hairsplitting, and it's no surprise that lawyers have long been heavily represented on the Executive Committee. In January 1934, for example, the Amateur Status Committee considered the case of "an advertisement containing a photo of Mrs. Nicholas Biddle, a member of the Huntington Valley Country Club in Philadelphia, endorsing a certain brand of cigarettes." The USGA's policy was not to look for infractions but to pass judgment on any potential violations brought to its attention. "The underlying question presented" by Mrs. Biddle was whether she had capitalized on her skill as a golfer. She appeared in the ad, the committee decided, "not on account of her golf playing, but rather on account of her social position and attractive appearance, and, therefore, no action should be taken in the matter."

Don Cherry was a popular singer who was a good enough golfer to play in the Amateur and Open, and to compete on Walker Cup teams. An advertisement referring to him as "the recording and singing golfer" came to the USGA's attention. Now if people were coming to see him sing *because* he was a golfer,

Tom Watson strokes an iron on Baltusrol's par-three fourth; he would finish tied for third in this 1980 Open at the New Jersey course.

Tony Roberts

he would lose his amateur status. But if he sang for his living, was he supposed to keep his golf a secret? Insurance salesmen could pitch a policy on the links without threatening their status, so why couldn't Don Cherry croon?

All this apparent captiousness contributed to a popular view of the USGA as a rather stuffy outfit, a constellation of aging preppies who strolled the championship grounds dressed as the prototypes for Ralph Lauren, men who took delight in setting up the Open course to humiliate the professionals and in ruining the game for the beer-and-a-shot set by forbidding the Calcutta. Gambling and prizes always gave the USGA fits, as it struggled to distinguish a friendly wager—essential to golf's joy but in no way a threat to one's amateur status—from private competitions where real treasures were buried. Like moral Masons and Dixons, the USGA surveyed the boundaries of propriety.

Treason is rare in the country of golf, where cheating in championships is unheard of and players call penalties on themselves, but flawed comportment is not unknown. Bobby Jones once injured a spectator with a thrown club and was famous for his temper. Eventually his chagrin at actually quitting in frustration over his inept play during the middle of a round in the British Open cured him of bad manners. He was thereafter the Paragon. The USGA once "noted with alarm the tendency of professionals to throw clubs," and vowed to keep an eye on Tommy Bolt when he came to Oakmont for the 1953 Open. Bolt, decorous at last, won the Open in 1958 at Southern Hills. Lee Trevino, the two-time Open champion with a genius for apt summary, caught the USGA's public image in his sights. "When I reach sixty," he said, "I'm gonna buy a blue blazer and a can of dandruff and run the USGA."

But the USGA, with a measured pace and an occasional stumble, walks to the music of time. Its force derives from consent, like all good government. Its Rules are hallowed, graced by the whisper of ancient voices. *Keep the game of golf clean.*

CHARLIE MACDONALD RODE BACK TO NEWPORT IN THE FALL of 1895 to play in the first Amateur, easily winning his first four eighteen-hole matches. No qualifying rounds had been necessary, there were so few entrants. In the thirty-six-hole final, he was twelve up with eleven to play—to this day, the greatest margin of victory in an Amateur final. Vindication, at long last—Charlie Macdonald was the one true Amateur champion. Then someone noticed that Macdonald and his opponent had each recruited a professional to "follow them over the course to coach them and advise, a questionable proceeding in what should be strictly amateur in every respect."

Committeeman!

1

The Competitive Game

To succeed, you can't be afraid to fail. To win, you've got to put yourself in a position to lose.—Curtis Strange

Playing it safe has never been the mark of a champion. A great golfer attacks the course, with mind and nerve and a body that could well humiliate him at the next dogleg. And when the impossible shot is pulled off—out of matted rough, from treacherous sand, or through a maze of trees—he hitches up his trousers and strides on, certain that *this* day will be his. He drives the ball farther on the next hole; the crowd roars and his pace down the fairway quickens. Across the course, the cheers and red numbers racing across scoreboards signal birdie after birdie.

Whether competing at stroke or match play, for a million-dollar pot or silver plate, the course is always the golfer's primary adversary. But, as Byron Nelson explained, "You have to have the drive to want to beat somebody, you have to be willing to dig down and discipline yourself to be better than somebody else." The masters of the game have been passionate about that.

For JoAnne Carner, who revels in intimidation, "Competition is even more fun than golf. I like going down to the wire knowing somebody's going to choke, and hoping it's not me."

AP/Wide World Photos

Trevor Jones/Phil Sheldon

2

The Bettmann Archive

3

Sam Snead relished the battles, particularly against both Nelson and Hogan. Half a century later he still can recount each of those rounds, blow by blow. Snead always searched an opponent's face and game for hints of weakness. Sometimes the evidence was all too obvious. In their 1940 PGA Championship playoff, Nelson, plagued by the nerves that would drive him into retirement by age thirty-four, vomited from the tension. Yet on that championship day at Hershey Country Club in Pennsylvania, Nelson held fast and bested Snead one-up in thirty-six holes. "But head-to-head in tournament play I got *Ben* every time," Snead boasts even now.

1 Sam Snead's shot from the rough finished six feet from the hole at the 1945 Los Angeles Open. He took the title.

2 John Daly chases an errant ball into the crowd at the 1993 British Open at Sandwich.

3 Arnold Palmer gets a chuckle out of Gary Player's plight in the 1963 Thunderbird Open.

Andy Levin

4

Focus on Sports

5

Larry Petrillo

6

4 *Consumed by the action at the 1993 Open at Baltusrol.*
5 *A caddie at the 1989 Open at Oak Hill.*
6 *For just the third time in sixty-eight years, Great Britain and Ireland capture the Walker Cup match in 1989 at Peachtree.*
7 *Patriots at the 1993 Open at Baltusrol.*
8 *Craig Stadler ponders his game at Pebble Beach.*
9 *Jack Nicklaus with Gary Player at the 1962 World Series of Golf.*
10 *Isao Aoki finished second to Jack Nicklaus at the 1980 Open.*
11 *Hall-of-Famer Nancy Lopez in 1978.*

Amy Janello

7

Mickey Pfleger

8

Bob Gomel/Life Magazine

9

Walter Iooss, Jr./Sports Illustrated

10

Ken Regan/Camera 5

11

12

USGA Collection

13

Bettmann/UPI

14

Andy Levin

15

Robert Walker

12 A spectator at the 1929 Open at Winged Foot gets a lift and a great view from a bamboo pole held by friendly marshals.
13 A grand old tee party in the American South.
14 A chef from a nearby service tent follows a player's drive at the 1993 Open.
15 Spectators stampede to see Curtis Strange top Nick Faldo in the playoff at the 1988 Open at The Country Club in Brookline.

Lawrence N. Levy/Yours In Sport

16

Leonard Kamsler

17

Bettmann/UPI

18

16 With thousands competing for a view at the Open, it's best to have a periscope—or shoulders to sit on.

17 At the 1965 PGA Championship, Laurel Valley Golf Club gives home pro Arnold Palmer a club jacket and a welcome.

18 Byron Nelson captured his nineteenth victory of 1945 at Glen Garden, the Fort Worth course where he caddied as a boy.

19 *Gene Sarazen celebrates his one-stroke 1922 Open win at Skokie Country Club in Illinois.*

20 *Crowd pleasers Ben Hogan, in his first start after his near-fatal accident, and Sam Snead at the 1950 Los Angeles Open. Snead won the playoff.*

21 *Greg Norman at the 1988 Open at Brookline. Norman withdrew in the second round after injuring his arm when his club hit a rock.*

22 *Nick Faldo in search of his ball at Pebble Beach's fourteenth hole during the 1992 Open. He never found it, and finished fourth.*

23 *Golf is news at the 1938 Open at Cherry Hills Country Club in Colorado. Dick Metz ultimately lost to Ralph Guldahl.*

The Bettmann Archive

19

Bettmann/UPI

20

Jacqueline Duvoisin/Sports Illustrated

22

Leonard Kamsler

21

USGA Collection

23

24 *Ben Hogan finds the rough at the 1956 Open at Oak Hill. Hogan and Julius Boros tied for second; Cary Middlecoff was the winner.*

25 *Cary Middlecoff rode a second-round 65 to a victory in the 1965 Masters, by seven strokes over Ben Hogan.*

26 *Defending champ Jack Nicklaus fails to repeat in the 1964 Masters.*

John G. Zimmerman/Sports Illustrated

24

Jay Leviton/Sports Illustrated

25

Jay Maisel

26

Andy Levin

27

Courtesy The Country Club

28

Focus on Sports

29

Rick Stewart/Allsport

30

27 Runner-up Payne Stewart at the 1993 Open.

28 Francis Ouimet mugs with caddie and fans after his stunning 1913 Open upset over Ted Ray and Harry Vardon.

29 Ray Floyd's pulled six-iron fronting the eleventh hole in the 1990 Masters playoff cost him the title. The official is former USGA president Will Nicholson.

30 Patty Sheehan and Juli Inkster at the 1992 Women's Open at Oakmont. Sheehan won the playoff, her first Open title after three near-misses.

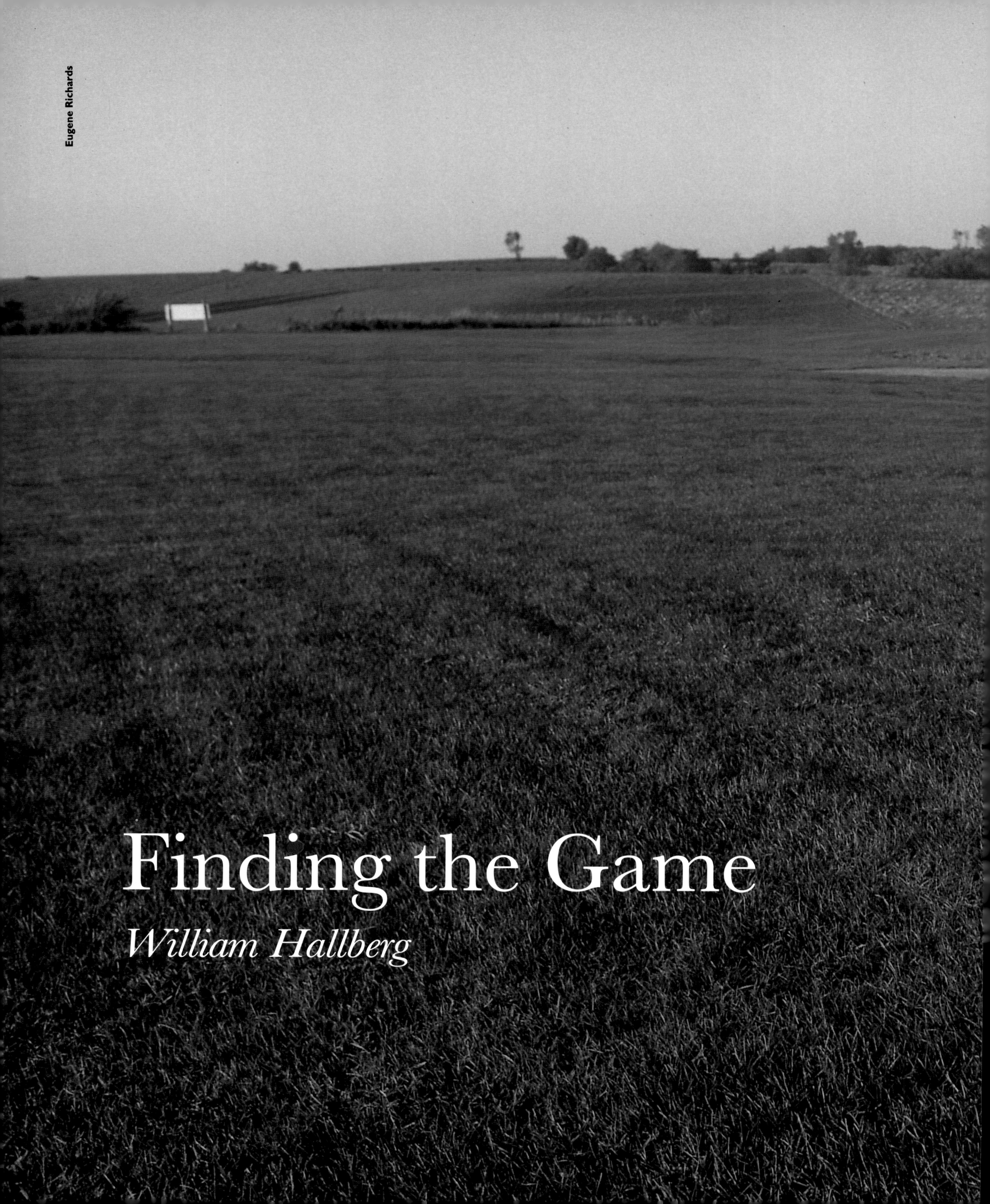

Eugene Richards

Finding the Game

William Hallberg

I N MY MIDWESTERN HOMETOWN, AT THE BOTTOM OF THE CAT-tail pond of the nine-hole university golf course, lay thousands of orphaned golf balls, each with its own tragic history: a shanked wedge that ruined the game of a lifetime; a topped five-wood that howled through the weedy perimeter into oblivion; a high-arcing pitch that soared optimistically toward a skullcap green beyond the footbridge, only to be captured by a wind gust and flipped into the drink. Through my dime-store diving goggles I saw among the crayfish and minnows old range balls with stripes around them so they looked like Saturn. There were pristine Titleists, Dots, and waterlogged Swan Floaters.

I was no golfer then. I was a scavenger, a comber of roughs and bushes, an entrepreneur. Every ball meant a quarter in my pocket, and golfers were just customers with twenty-five cents to spend.

In the evenings, from my perch in an elm tree, I watched them out there on the twilit fairways. Sound carried beautifully in the hours before dusk, when the wind was down. Every splash, every groan, every crack of ball against bark meant another quarter for me. I watched as codgers in green pants and heavy women in orange pedal pushers probed the roughs for lost balls. I did not climb down from my tree to help them.

When autumn came, few golfers ventured onto the course. Its fairways became football grounds for neighborhood kids. The forsythias framing the number five green served as end-zone markers. The pole-top martin houses flanking the tee were the opposite goal. If we made way for the occasional cool-weather golfer, it was grudgingly, and we wished him ill. We laughed when his sliced drive landed on Wooster Street and bounced out of sight. We had no reverence for the game.

The ponds froze solid by January and stayed frozen until March. Enter skaters and snowballers and broomstick hockey players, filling the golf-course landscape like peasants in a Brueghel painting. Presbyterian elders built pondside fires, roasted hot dogs, and led the Youth Fellowship in hot-cocoa songs about being happy in the snow. Nobody gave a thought to the game that waited, latent beneath the snow.

Leonard Kamsler

Previous spread: At Essex Golf Club, one of more than two hundred nine-hole Iowa courses, this boy has boundless horizons.

An onlooker (above) studies the competition at the 1961 Pee Wee championship.

Leonard Kamsler

I "found" golf shortly after the last crest of snow melted on the course. It was a mid-March day—a Saturday, early in the morning—with robins and yellow forsythia and moist, warm air blowing across the fairways. With nothing much in mind, I pilfered a five-iron from my dad's set of yellow-shafted Spalding Bobby Jones golf clubs hanging near the hot-water heater in the garage. I also took two Maxflis from the zippered pouch of his plaid bag. Then, across the street to the number six fairway. I found a perfect spot on the tee, dropped a ball on the grass, took a stance, drew the club back, and swung hard. The result was miraculous. The ball flew into the blue sky, hovered beautifully there, then fell onto the middle of the fairway. I will never forget the sound of the clubface making solid contact with the ball, or the magical feel of it. In my mind's eye, that tiny sphere will hang against the cloudless sky forever. I had found the game.

DISCOVERING GOLF DOES NOT ALWAYS OCCUR ON IDYLLIC tracts of land during the romance of youth, nor do the game's mysteries reveal themselves in a single, breathtaking moment. Sometimes the process takes years; there are god-awful days on the fairways and greens and practice grounds—and it is the indignities you suffer on those days that bring you back to the number one tee week after week. "I'm not *this* bad," you mutter. "Nobody is *this* bad." Still, you shank and dribble and duck-hook. You curse your stupidity and incompetence. And you mean it. Finally, in despair, you check out instruction books, you carve divots in your front yard, you shell out money for lessons. In due course, your drives begin to land on the short grass, and your putts begin to fall. You are nice to your spouse again, and life regains its sweetness.

There are, of course, plenty of golfers for whom finding the game has little to do with mastering it; what they cherish is the camaraderie. The green fairways, the swoosh of the ball washer, the click of cleats on asphalt cart paths induce an openness that can't be found anywhere else. Between the bogeys and golf talk, life's problems find air. Love lives are revealed; gossip spills out like shag balls from a canvas bag; then, on the heels of the most intimate revelation, you suddenly burst into laughter as your partner's shot ricochets off a green bench and hops out of bounds: a fine little metaphor for the vicissitudes of life. Later, on the eighteenth hole, you sweat over a putt that, if missed, will cost you and your partner a quarter. But the dreaded yips own your soul, and the cup seems as unattainable as the grail. There is a gleeful demonstration when, miraculously, the putt rattles inside the hole: high fives, moonwalking, clenched fists raised on high. Even your opponents are amused. These are the best times and the best friends you will ever have, and the golf course is the green ground that nourishes such friendships.

Pee Wee contestants and parents focus on a soaring tee shot.

The Bettmann Archive

And then there are those lovers of the game who never set foot on a golf course, but for whom the world stops on Saturday and Sunday afternoons when the Western Open or The Masters or the Ryder Cup or the Dinah Shore is on the tube. These sedentary golf fanatics have the complete bio and Sony Ranking of every player. They can tell you who is number forty-six on the money list and why Player X has missed five straight cuts. While they couldn't drop a two-foot putt, they are living proof that at least some of golf's mysteries can be appreciated from the cushiony comfort of a Broyhill sofa.

The legends of the game, meanwhile, have found their sport in all sorts of ways and places: caddie shacks, pastures, driving ranges, and makeshift golf courses carved into front lawns. Lee Trevino learned as a kid that golf was a way to make money: He made bets with wealthy men whose bags he carried at the Dallas Athletic Club, then he wagered his winnings that he could outplay the young African-American caddies who hung around the caddie shack. There were three holes behind the shack, and that's where the contest took place. "As soon as one of us would hit, he'd throw the club to another guy." Golf clubs were "flying around." The love of competition became ingrained, and Trevino's brilliance as a golfer began to emerge.

Nancy Lopez was a kid tagging along behind her parents at a hard-baked municipal course in Houston when, on a whim, her dad handed her a four-wood and a ball from his wife's bag. "Hit it," he told his daughter, "and hit it again until you reach the green." Well, she nearly beaned her parents with a ball that whizzed between their skulls.

Ted Rhodes, a golfer of the 1940s and 1950s, learned the game by hitting golf balls on the grounds of a public park in Memphis, aiming his shots at twigs stuck in the ground. Sam Snead used maple branches to fashion his own clubs when he was growing up in West Virginia. Bobby Jones, who grew up in Atlanta, created a miniature golf course in his front yard, burying tin cans all over the lawn. He used a sawed-off cleek and counted

Aaron Chang

Twelve-year-old entrepreneur Julius Hamilton of Ozone Park, New York (top, left), opened his own "Rinkiedink Golf Course." Green fees: two cents.

At Honolulu's Ala Wai Golf Club (left), eight-year-old Brett Asato agonizes over a miss as his dad, Clyde, looks on.

Morning four-ball (above) at Van Cortlandt Park in the Bronx, New York.

every stroke, an intimation of the integrity that marked his career. Babe Didrikson Zaharias, having outrun and outjumped everybody on the planet, took up golf because it looked so easy. It wasn't, not even for the greatest female athlete in history. She practiced until her hands bled, day after day, for years, until she felt ready to compete. Jack Nicklaus would probably never have picked up a golf club if his dad hadn't sustained a foot injury for which golf was the prescribed therapy. Jack tagged along for a while, carrying his father's clubs, then out of boredom decided to join in. If everyone who took up the game played his or her early golf, as Nicklaus did, on a Donald Ross masterpiece like Scioto Country Club in Columbus, Ohio, millions more American golfers would be traipsing the nation's fairways.

Some of us grew up playing on a manicured country club course; others launched our golf careers in fading light on a ragged municipal course. Each of us found the game in our own way—and our love of it is as strong as that of any touring professional.

The amazing strength of our devotion is evident in metropolitan areas from coast to coast, where devotees queue up at mad morning hours to play eighteen holes—"Foursomes Only, Carts Required," say the signs—on terribly overcrowded courses. At Bethpage State Park's five-course complex on Long Island, where *all* members of a foursome must purchase a ticket before a tee-off time can be assigned, lines start to form at 3:30 a.m. Jerry

Loosening up at first light on the first tee. At Bethpage Black on Long Island, players arrive at 3:30 a.m. to be assigned tee times.

De Croce, a retired liquor store owner, is one of the course rangers. He politely keeps the traffic moving. You can kick around briefly in the tall grass for your errant Top Flite, but you are always aware of a ranger eyeing you from his cart. Here a lost ball is *definitely* a lost ball. "Oh, well," you say.

During the Depression, Jerry bused tables at Woodmere Country Club, a few miles down the road from Bethpage, then switched to carrying golf clubs at $1.50 per bag. Sometimes he shouldered two sets of clubs, which made for a lot of slaloming across the fairway from one client to the other. On Mondays, he recalls, the course was open to caddies, but he had no clubs. "Then I found a used set—a wood, four irons, and a putter. All of that for $6. So then I could play. My friends would say, 'How can you chase around a white ball all day?' and I'd ask them, 'How can you enjoy hanging a piece of string over the side of a boat?' " Returning from wartime military service in Europe, Jerry opened his store and played golf with his brothers after supper until it grew too dark to play. "I loved the camaraderie. It was something we could do together, besides work."

In 1954 he met and married "a pretty Scottish girl," Christine Morris Sinclair, with whom he plays golf every week or so. On several occasions, the two have played in Great Britain, most often at Royal Troon and Hexham-on-Tyne, where, he recalls, the fescue grass on the green was so long that four-putts were common. Now Jerry, who wears a tam o'shanter at all times, can play golf five days a week, Monday through Friday. He leaves the weekends for working people—"That's *their* time, not mine"—but he's still there, rangering, "trying to make golf more fun for everybody, even if I have to grump at the slowpokes now and then." He especially enjoys working with the kids who frequent the courses in the afternoons: "I help them with their games. That's the thrill for me. For me, *that's* finding the game."

In many families, golf is an essential part of the father-son relationship, a means of bonding as well as a rite of initiation into the adult world. Father and son find each other as the son finds the game. Take Tom Friedman, for example. He learned golf from his dad, an executive in the ball-bearing business. Most of Tom's summertime hours were spent at the Minneapolis Country Club where his family were members. After his father finished work in the late afternoon, the two of them would grab a bite of supper, then hurry out to play a round of golf before twilight. It was during those long golden hours when the northern sun would not go down that father and son talked about politics and religion and the social issues affecting the world outside the clean, prosperous city in which they lived. "I could easily have believed that the entire planet was just like my own hometown if it were not for what I learned out there on the course," Friedman says. "I learned as much about life as I did about golf."

One of the highlights of Tom's youth was when he was

Bettmann/UPI

chosen from a lottery to be one of a few dozen high school kids who would caddie for the pros at the 1970 Open at Hazeltine. Tom drew Chi Chi Rodriguez.

A dozen years later, he had exchanged the tranquillity of Minnesota for the terrors of Beirut, where even donkeys might explode at any moment. As a reporter for *The New York Times*, Thomas L. Friedman spent a decade in one of the world's most dangerous cities. His reporting won him two Pulitzer Prizes, and in 1989 his book *From Beirut to Jerusalem* won the National Book Award.

So what did Friedman do for relaxation amid the exploding bombs and artillery fire? He frequented the most vulnerable, wide-open patch of earth in the city, the Beirut Golf and Country Club. "The golfers at the Beirut Club didn't call the first hole a dangerous par five for nothing," Friedman says. "Several members were hit by bullets in their backswings there because the 460-yard hole ran perpendicular to a PLO firing range. I was actually relieved when my ball went into a sand bunker; it was the safest place on the course."

Instead of aiming their tee shots at some distant oak tree or barn, Tom and his partners—mostly diplomats, journalists, and military officers—would often target a plume of black smoke rising on the horizon or a solitary soldier on a nearby hill, an assault rifle slung over his shoulder. Friedman recalls that on his periodic visits to Israel, the Christian and Shi'ite militia would stop him at the checkpoints because they couldn't believe that any man would be carrying something as innocent as a set of Wilson Staffs on his shoulder. They tried twisting the head off his pitching wedge to see if any bullets or contraband were inside the shaft. They unzipped the pocket of his bag, sending balls "bouncing all over the customs hall."

Now the *Times*'s White House correspondent, Friedman is able to play golf every week at his home course, Caves Valley, in the Maryland countryside just outside the Beltway. He often remembers those evenings in Minnesota when, marching alongside his father, he found the game. "Even though my dad died

Scott Thode

During a lull in Beirut's Shi'ite–Christian skirmishing in 1983, leatherneck Mike Clepper hones his explosion shot (top, left).

Chi Chi Rodriguez (above), via his Florida-based foundation, brings the joy of the game to hundreds of troubled kids.

several years ago," he says, "I can't play a round of golf without imagining he's there with me."

Erik Pack is a twenty-five-year-old executive for a New York entertainment company who, like Friedman, owes his interest in golf to his father. In Erik's case, though, it wasn't so much the game or the companionship that appealed to him; it was the thrill of piloting a golf cart at a public course some thirty miles outside of Los Angeles: "Sometimes I'd go too fast through the trees or I'd drive in front of somebody who was just about to hit. I was ten years old, and I was *driving* something!"

A few years later his father, a television advertising executive, got tickets to the Bob Hope Desert Classic, where the two of them followed Gary Player and Tom Watson. "We'd watch them hit these impossible shots. They'd think nothing of it. They were having a good time," Erik recalls.

Just after Christmas that year, Erik and a friend scraped together two sets of mismatched clubs and strolled over to the public course with Christmas money in their pockets. "It was early morning, and we were just going to play nine holes, then go home for lunch. At a public course they always put you in a foursome, so they stuck us with these two unlucky guys who were going to play eighteen." It took hours to play nine holes, Erik says, and while the boys dug divots and bounced golf balls off prickly pear cactuses, the two grown-ups waved through foursome after foursome: country-and-western quartets, ladies in neon attire, oldsters in straw hats. "We had a lot of fun that day," Erik says, "but you couldn't really call it golf."

The following year, Erik's father moved the family from Los Angeles to New York. His father joined Sleepy Hollow Country Club in nearby Scarborough, and Erik's interest in golf soon grew into a passion. "I would play the smaller, nine-hole course with my new friends every day of every summer," he remembers. "*Every single day.*" He took lessons from the club pro, and his game suddenly and dramatically improved. "That was maybe when I found the game. It began to make sense to me: If your hands did this, the blade would do that; if your head came up, the ball stayed low. The game had a wonderful logic. I couldn't get enough of it. I loved it."

During his junior year in high school, Erik rebelled "against the sameness you find everywhere" and adopted a punk look: "You know, green hair and all that, and I wore engineer boots with handcuffs attached and a leather jacket and a Mohawk, which I thought was very amusing, especially with me being on the high school golf team." Occasionally, the tournaments would be held at exclusive private clubs, and sometimes the members didn't much like Erik's new look.

On one such occasion, at a private club in Westchester, the Sleepy Hollow team piled out of the coach's station wagon—and there was Erik with full Mohawk and heavy boots. The

Leonard Kamsler

Moral support from Mom at the Pee Wee Nationals (above).

Ben Hogan (right) with his admirers at the 1942 Hale America National Open, a tournament that replaced the U.S. Open during World War II and helped raise money for the Allied effort.

Mohawk was allowed; not so the boots, which would damage the greens. The coach of the opposing team offered Erik a pair of shoes two sizes too small; Erik wore them anyway. "Except for the conventional-looking shoes, I was my own frightening self."

Erik was the last of his team's players to finish. On the number eight hole, his coach warned him of a surprise that was in store for him. "When I got to number nine tee, I saw in the distance that the entire green was surrounded by people: my teammates, the other team, caddies, big shots, the maître d', bathroom attendants. They had all come out to see this guy with the nine-inch green Mohawk and earrings. Coach was pretty amused. I was a little nervous. I felt like I was in a professional tournament or something. There was an audience.

"My approach shot was an eight-iron, and I hit probably the finest shot of my life and landed maybe two inches from the pin. Everyone standing around the green applauded. And my coach, he was ecstatic. That was my best moment in golf. I was going through this phase where I looked like a weirdo, but I was still able to say something to the people in a very graceful way, which was a good feeling."

Erik, who now lives in a Brooklyn apartment, says he

USGA Collection

Seny Norasingh

doesn't know "whether I found golf or it found me," but in any case "I have a personal relationship with the sport. It's *my* thing, *my* game. It's a relationship I have with a golf ball, and a course, and my clubs. I'll always want to play golf, no matter where I am."

When he's older and more settled, Erik says he'll make a putting green in his backyard. "I'll play until I'm one hundred. . . if I can still swing a club."

NO GOLFING PARENT HELPED MARTHA FILES FIND GOLF; ARNOLD Palmer lent a hand, in a way that could only have happened in an American home in the second half of the twentieth century. Martha was thirteen years old and sitting cross-legged in front of a black-and-white TV set in her parents' house in Durham, North Carolina, when, in 1970 she fell in love with Arnold Palmer. "I guess I liked the way he turned his head horizontal after he hit a shot," Martha says. "Like he was looking at something pretty amazing. A car wreck, a UFO. And he always walked as if he'd just won the lottery. And I thought he was good-looking, too."

Martha's stepfather, who died when she was a teenager, would sometimes watch with her. He reinforced her admiration for Palmer and her doubts about Nicklaus. "Look at him," he would say as Nicklaus stood over a putt. "He's going to miss. Takes too long. See? *Now,* watch Arnie."

Martha decided that if she ever took up golf, she would play the Palmer way. She would hitch up her breeches and cock her head and "squinch up" her face, too. And she would hit the ball *hard.* Although her stepfather knew next to nothing about golf, he knew that Martha was fascinated by the sport, so he bought her a junior set of Wilson Sam Snead woods and irons. She promptly started to practice in the family's small backyard. "I learned my golf from the *World Book Encyclopedia,*" Martha says. "Back then, the interlocking grip was in style, so I imitated all the diagrams until I was a bona fide *World Book* prototype." The encyclopedia provided a rudimentary discussion of the Rules of the game, and Martha committed them to memory.

It was only after a couple of years of backyard golf that her

Nakia Davis (top, left) has been competing since she was eleven. Her father's uncles and cousins laughed when he began to teach Davis the game. "They said he was wasting his time," she says. "I guess we showed them."

Arnold Palmer (right) captured the 1962 British Open at Royal Troon in Scotland. Television helped make Arnie the King, perhaps the most popular golfer ever.

Brian Seed/Sports Illustrated

Uncle Robert, a construction worker and former semipro baseball player, took her out to a nearby public course for her first round. "I was thrilled to be out there, even though I shot about a million," Martha says, adding that her uncle's baseball past lived on in the way he strangled his golf club. "He even putted with that grip."

In high school Martha wanted to play on the boys' golf team. When she asked the coach if she could join, he suggested cheerleading. "I was hurt and angry and determined to become as good as the boys, even if I couldn't play on the team," Martha says. "I checked out instruction books, took lessons, absorbed everything. I practiced like a maniac."

These days, when she isn't traveling the Carolinas selling easels, portable blackboards, and overhead projectors, Martha Files frequents the lush fairways of her Rees Jones-designed home course, Emerald Golf Club in New Bern, North Carolina. "If I can't play, I practice; if I can't practice, I fantasize. That's how bad I've got the bug," she says.

In 1992, at Durham's Occoneechee Country Club, she made her first hole-in-one; the following year she won the Emerald

USGA Collection

Seny Norasingh

After advancing to the quarterfinals at the 1938 Women's Amateur, Patty Berg (left) takes time out to sign autographs for the Westmoreland Country Club caddie corps.

"Without golf, we'd be going different directions," says Tim Miller (above), on the range at Pinehurst with his son Chris. "It was the same with me and my father."

Golf Club Ladies Invitational. "I felt like somebody else was swinging the club; it was your basic out-of-body experience—and my best experience on a golf course by far. It really fired me up to drastically improve my game. I know it's a cliché, but golf really *is* a lot like life. There are bad things and good things that happen, but you just keep on trucking."

Major Stephen Jones, alias "the Captain," is the son of a painting contractor in Ahoskie, North Carolina, a man who, Stephen says, "never so much as touched a golf club from the day he was born to the day he died. He worked too hard."

As a boy, Stephen played tennis: "But when I joined the Army in 1971, nobody seemed to play tennis, at least nobody at my rank. So I took up golf, on the driving range mostly."

He got his first "real look" at the game when he and some of his Army buddies drove up I-95 from Fort Bragg to an all-African-American tournament held at Hickory Meadows, a smalltown North Carolina club. "This was the Chitlin Circuit, the barbecue tour, and they weren't playing for a lot of money, but you'd never know it. They went after the game with such intensity. They did a lot of talking, but they backed it up when they hit the ball. I mean, some of those guys could kill their drives. Then they'd stride down the fairway with this look of supreme confidence. Those guys had so much style and pride. They were the 'gunfighters' who just came into a town somewhere and gambled they could beat the best player around, white or black, which they almost always did. Guys like Robert "Eyes" Pettis, probably the best putter in the world. But now they were playing in a real competitive tournament, and they were dressed in the fanciest clothes you could ever imagine—yellow slacks and shoes all polished. They walked the walk and talked the talk. I was really proud to see them. I wanted to emulate their style. Even now, I always dress well when I'm on the course."

The Captain first played golf at Tong Du Chon Golf Club, up in the mountains of South Korea. After spending a few months "burning worms" and "digging holes" in and around the fairway, he took a lesson from a Korean pro named Mister Pae, whose only English was the phrase "Too much downward blow." While stationed in Korea, Stephen boarded the "golf bus" at 5:30 a.m., four times a week, and he played with anybody who showed up at the clubhouse. Sometimes, if he was paired with a Korean, neither of them uttered a word: "Just a lot of peculiar gestures, you know, the international sign language of golf. Everybody knows 'choke' and that shrug when you hit one out of bounds."

Golf soon became a real obsession for the Captain, who now plays the Officer's Club course at Fort Bragg. "What really thrills me about golf," he says, "is the people who play the game. I mean, at some of the courses you can feel like an outsider if you're black. But once you're on the course, people are people. Strange how that works." Nowadays, he says, he plays only with African-

American friends. "We're like a subculture, and it's comfortable for us. All of us know who the great black golfers are—like 'Tex' Gillory and Teddy Rhodes. We've seen them all play, or we've caddied for them or played with them. Gillory was Army, you know."

During a stint in the ROTC unit at East Carolina University in Greenville, North Carolina, Stephen spent his free afternoons teaching youngsters how to swing the golf clubs he had salvaged for them at junk shops and garage sales. He believes some of them will stick with—and, in time, excel at—the sport.

Recently, too, he bought a set of Bullet golf clubs for his two young sons and took them to a par-three course in Fayetteville. There, instead of worrying them about their swings, he taught them to fix divots, to stay out of each other's line, and to shoot in turn. "I want them to revere the game the way I do. I want them to enjoy it as much as I do. I practice for hours every week, because it gives me pleasure. I could *live* at the practice range. When I can't golf, I think about it or read about it or dream about it. I want to be a great golfer yet—or die trying."

David Bennett lives only minutes from the Baltusrol Golf Club, in New Jersey, the site of the 1993 U.S. Open. Ever since 1936, when he was fifteen years old, David has been a local volunteer at Baltusrol, helping to make the five Opens held there since then, and other events, run smoothly. "The U.S. Open is a momentous tournament, and Baltusrol is a majestic course. I love feeling as if I'm a part of the drama and history, however small a part that might be." At the 1993 event, he manned a leader board, flipping the numbers that added up to success or failure for the players whose names appeared or dropped out of sight.

David came to Baltusrol—and to golf—by way of his father, Charles, a certified public accountant who immigrated from Burton-on-Trent, England, in the 1920s. By the mid-1930s, the immigrant was a member in good standing at Baltusrol, and it was de rigueur for members to lend assistance when the club hosted a major event. So in 1936 Charles Bennett was keeping score for the pairing of Tony Manero, the eventual winner of a fierce struggle for the title, and Gene Sarazen.

David assisted his father and recalls watching in "total awe" as the competition boiled, then simmered, then boiled again on a hot New Jersey afternoon: "Things were different then. The players said almost nothing. Not to the galleries, and certainly not to each other. There were no fools yelling, *'You're the man!'* You didn't need ropes to keep the gallery back." David was used to seeing his father punch his drives off the tee. These fellows *murdered* the ball. "It was a wholly different game, exciting and dramatic."

Later that summer Charles Bennett's accounting firm was contracted by Wisconsin's largest Menomonee Indian Reservation to oversee a deal with a big lumber company. There, to the amazement of father and son, they found an eighteen-hole golf

Courtesy Golf Digest

Golf pro Ted Rhodes and boxing heavyweight champ Joe Louis keep a keen eye on Joe, Jr., as he tees it up.

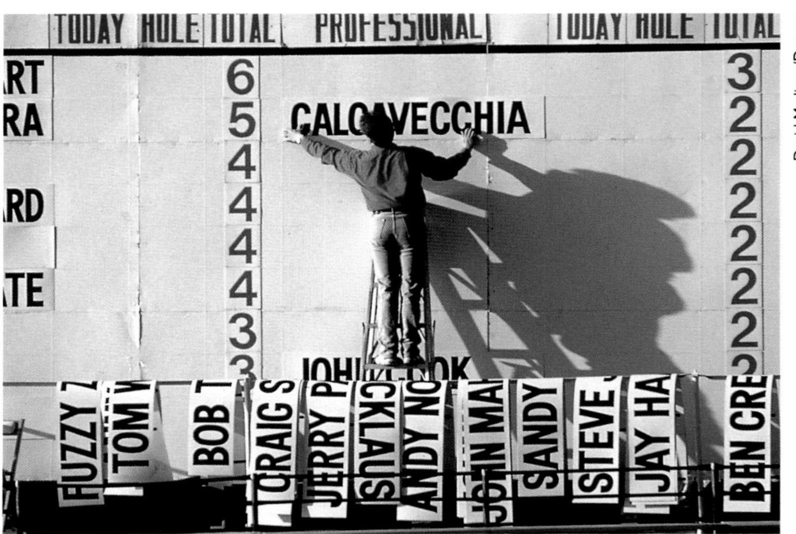

David Madison/Duomo

course "cut right into the birches and pines of the reservation." It was there, where Charles Bennett felt less concerned about digging divots than he would have on Baltusrol's pristine fairways, that he initiated his son in the mysteries of the game. "Dad taught me the pendulum putting stroke. He'd say, 'By Jove, that's it, son.' " He bought David a set of MacGregor Tourney clubs that summer, and when they returned to New Jersey he insisted that David take lessons from Johnny Farrell, the legendary Baltusrol club pro and world-renowned teacher. "That was when I really learned to play the game—and to *appreciate* it. The better I got, the more I knew how difficult the game was.

"My dad and I had a great day together a couple of years later when he broke eighty during a match with me and a couple of friends," David recalls, adding, "That was the only time I recall his having shot a score in the seventies. He was a very reserved man, my father, and all he said afterward was 'Splendid! It was splendid fun. Absolutely splendid.' "

In 1940 David went off to Duke University—and then to war, flying combat missions over Germany as a bombardier. It was only when he got back home, he says, that he really found golf.

"I practiced like crazy after I got back, and so did my old high school pals—Homer, Larry, and John. They'd also seen a lot of action overseas. We teed off on the Lower Course at Baltusrol one Sunday afternoon. Larry was a scratch golfer and John was about a two handicap, as was Homer. I was the weak link at five or thereabouts. After nine holes we were, *all* of us, *under* par, with me in the lead. We looked at each other after our putts and laughed until there were tears in our eyes. Maybe we knew the war was finally over; I can't tell you for sure, but that was my best moment on a golf course."

A few years later David played his last round with his father. Electric carts were banned from the course in those days, and he recalls having to put a hand on his father's back to help him up the Baltusrol hills. "It was an odd thing and very sad. I knew that this was it for him. His golfing days were over, but he took it with his typical stiff upper lip. Still, he had many, many happy years playing his brand of golf. I hope I'm as lucky as he in that respect."

Andy Levin

Like a highway billboard, this monster sign (top, left) at a PGA tournament gives galleries the scores from far off.

Full bleachers are the rule at Opens, here at Baltusrol Golf Club (above). Attendance for the 1993 event topped 170,000.

Two players stroll down the fairway at Cleveland Metro Park (above).

At Cedarbrook Golf Club near Philadelphia, 1950s caddies trail their players (top, right).

Misha Erwitt

Archive Photos/Lambert

WHETHER WE FIND THE GAME AS THE SONS OR DAUGHTERS OF golfing parents or are drawn to it by the images of golf's masters competing on TV, the game rewards us with a happiness that more than compensates for its moments of frustration and despair. It is, in every sense, a generous game and true companion to those of any age.

Now, as I write, the air is taking on the crispness of fall. It won't be long before, back in the midwestern town where I grew up, people my age who have played golf all summer will shiver and decide it's time to leave the fairways to the neighborhood kids. The ponds will freeze solid, and for a season, the game will wait, latent beneath the snow, to be discovered by another generation of youngsters. Among them there will surely be at least one who will never forget the sight of that first high-arcing ball whose path suggests a vital new dimension that can take a lifetime to explore.

Robert Walker

The Architect's Vision

Tom Doak

***Previous spread:* Hard by the Pacific, Pebble Beach's 431-yard par-four eighth hole demands one of the most exacting approach shots in the game.**

The sixteenth at Cypress Point (above): the most heroic carry in golf.

Focus on Sports

*O*CTOBER *1928:* DR. *ALISTER MACKENZIE,* THE *GLOBE-trotting Scottish golf architect, sits atop a grassy knoll at Crystal Downs, a small residential community in northern Michigan, a bottle of Scotch by his side. "I have the plan for the front nine," he tells his assistant, Perry Maxwell. "Come see what you think of it." After studying the plan, Maxwell tells Mackenzie that he likes every one of the holes, but that there are only eight of them. Thus, the green of the ninth hole, a classic uphill par three, was crowded onto the ridgetop where the two men sat. A few days later, with the routing complete and Maxwell armed with rough sketches of his designs for the greens, Mackenzie resumes his journey from California to England.*

April 1988: Paul "Pete" Dye is on his knees in the desert of Tempe, Arizona, at work on the creation of the Karsten Golf Course for Arizona State University. Dye's oldest son, Perry, is the architect of record for the new course, but the father is the star attraction, surrounded by an entourage of project managers and university VIPs whenever he makes a site visit. The group huddles to listen as Dye instructs a bulldozer operator on the design of the par-three twelfth hole:

"We've got it all wrong here. Let me show you what I want to do. Build it up more over on this side and let the green tilt down to the left," Dye says, molding the dirt in front of him with his hands into a rough model of the green site. "Cut a deep bunker on the front left—six or seven feet down. Then jazz up the approach on the right with some rolls and mounds to tie it in with the mounding on that side of the green, and try to sneak the cart path to thirteen through those mounds, so you can't see it from the tee. Understand?" The shaper nods. As Dye gets up to dust himself off, he scuffs at the dirt with his foot, destroying the evidence of his thoughts.

ONE OF THE JOYS OF GOLF ARCHITECTURE IS THAT, AS TOM Fazio delights in saying, "There are no rules of golf-course design"—no minimum or maximum length of hole, no enforced limit of contouring to greens or bunkers, no guidebook for the placing of hazards. Unlike other sports whose playing fields are rigidly defined, golf courses are so big that it is impossible to standardize them.

In Scotland, where the game evolved on coastal land, the sandy ground was shaped by the wind and the rain, and the early

USGA Collection

courses were determined by locating the best patches of turf on which to hole out, then finding the path of least resistance from one "green" to the next. Indeed, before the age of tourism and competitive golf, golfers of different towns evolved different styles of play based on their home courses—the St. Andrews man had a long, free swing because the wide course did not punish free swinging, while the North Berwick native had a short, wristy stroke conducive to playing approaches to its small and tricky greens.

As golf's popularity spread from Scotland to England and then overseas, at around the turn of the century, courses often had to be built on land that was not ideally suited to the game. Accordingly, the terrain was adapted to the architect's vision of play. As a result, America's great playing fields—from Augusta National, with manicured turf almost everywhere, to Pine Valley, where the New Jersey Pine Barrens encroach on every tee and every fairway—have personalities as distinctive as those of the men who shaped them.

One of the most colorful personalities in the field was Alister Mackenzie. A veteran of the Boer War, during which he learned to appreciate the native art of camouflage, Mackenzie built courses from Moortown, England, to Royal Melbourne, Australia, distinguished by their bold and beautiful bunkers and rolling greens that blended into the surrounding terrain.

Before pursuing his avocation of golf-course design, Mackenzie had practiced as a medical doctor in Leeds, England. He justified his change of profession on the basis of his "firm conviction of the extraordinary influence on health of pleasurable excitement, especially when combined with fresh air and exercise." To follow through with this noble goal in his golf-course designs, he sought to provide "the greatest good for the greatest number of golfers," in terms of enjoying the course. Late in his career, Dr. Mackenzie collaborated with the peerless Bobby Jones on the design of Augusta National.

Jones later elaborated on their shared philosophy. "There are two ways of widening the gap between a good shot and a bad one," he observed. "One is to inflict a severe and immediate punishment upon the bad shot, to place its perpetrator in a bunker

Robert Walker

The architectural use of timber supports is nothing new. Witness these revetments at the fifteenth at North Berwick in Scotland (top, left), built in the 1870s.

Set among the Pine Barrens of central New Jersey, Pine Valley Golf Club (above) has often been judged the world's best golf course. Holes like the par-three tenth severely punish inaccuracy.

Robert Walker

or in some other trouble demanding the sacrifice of a stroke in recovering; the other is to reward the good shot by making the second simpler in proportion to the excellence of the drive."

The latter philosophy of golf-course design—the one espoused by Mackenzie and Jones—came to be called the "strategic school," as opposed to the "penal school," which directly punished bad shots. It represented a revolutionary change, because up to that time most golf architects had come from the ranks of celebrated golfers—former Open champions like Willie Park, Jr., and James Braid and successful amateurs like Charles Blair Macdonald and William Fownes—for whom it was only natural to believe that a bad stroke deserved to be counted against one. Fownes summed up this philosophy nicely as he set about designing the Oakmont Country Club near Pittsburgh, Pennsylvania: "A shot poorly played should be a shot irrevocably lost."

Unlike their predecessors, who simply placed bunkers left and right of the line to the hole to catch off-line shots and cross-bunkers for topped drives, Macdonald, Fownes, and company did seek to introduce optional routes of play into their designs to create tactical interest; but the penalty for a misstep was usually severe. Macdonald explained his sternly moralistic reasoning to Grantland Rice in 1924: "I believe in leaving a way open for the player who can only drive one hundred yards, if he can keep that drive straight. But the one I am after is the golfer who thinks he can carry 180 yards when 160 yards is his limit. . . .This helps to make

Pull your drive left on either the third or fourth holes at Oakmont, and you'll find your ball in William Fownes's infamous "church pew" bunkers (above).

In Augusta, Georgia, the pine-studded Fruitlands Nursery was converted into Augusta National by Bobby Jones (below, with site plans) and Alister Mackenzie. Jones wanted the course to epitomize the strategic school of architecture.

The final hole at Augusta National (right) is all uphill; fairway bunkers penalize a drive too far left, and greenside sand swallows short or pushed approaches.

Acme Photos

Leonard Kamsler

John Biever/Sports Illustrated

a man know and study his limitations, and, if he is inclined to conceit, he will find his niblick has drawn a hard day's work."

Whatever their differences, practitioners of both schools share a deep understanding and love for the game. It is almost impossible to design good golf courses without a profound appreciation for all the shots in the good golfer's arsenal, because the success of the course is defined by how it plays. And penalists and strategists agree on a number of points. Mackenzie and Macdonald codified the essentials of an ideal course in their respective books on the subject: Both maintained that good land for golf was paramount; that artificial features should be naturalized to the greatest possible extent; that there should be the greatest possible variety of one-, two-, and three-shot holes; that any hazard was fair as long as an alternate route was provided around it for the weaker player; that walking between greens and tees should be minimized; and that the greens should be gently undulating in character and perfect in condition.

Although the architect must appreciate these and other aspects of good golf, he does not need to be able to play all the shots himself. Seth Raynor, for example, Macdonald's most successful protégé, refused on principle to play the game, because he believed his courses would get too easy if he worried about the average player. "The golfer must learn to play the ideal links," he declared, "and the ideal links should not come down to the playing ability of the average golfer." This, of course, speaks volumes about the force of his mentor's personality. So, too, does the fact that Raynor, a Princeton-educated engineer, took Macdonald's notes of famous British holes and, without ever having seen the models for his work at first hand, reproduced them on sites from Fishers Island in New York to Waialae in Honolulu.

Raynor was an exception. Most architects play as often as they can and, as might be expected, have tended to build courses along the lines of their own game. C. B. Macdonald's first layout for Chicago Golf Club had out-of-bounds to the left on all eighteen holes—just the opposite of his beloved St. Andrews, where the boundaries are nearly all to the right—but Macdonald tended to fade from the tee, so it was only natural for him to punish

Larry Perrillo

The 485-yard, par-five thirteenth (top, left), ringed by azaleas, bunkers, and Rae's Creek, is the climax of Amen Corner, the three holes in the far reaches of Augusta National.

Prairie Dunes Country Club in Hutchinson, Kansas (above), a Perry and Press Maxwell design, is reminiscent of links-style courses.

If players want to hit the green at the 535-yard par-five twelfth at Winged Foot's West Course (above), they had better be straight; A. W. Tillinghast's greenside bunkers are deep and penal, and the putting surface is narrow.

Rules expert and former USGA president Richard Tufts (top right, on left) and Donald Ross of Dornoch, Scotland. Ross, a legendary architect, served as pro at Tufts's Pinehurst Resort and Country Club until his death in 1948.

Leonard Kamsler

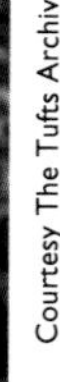

Courtesy The Tufts Archives

the hook, which he saw as a wild and uncontrolled shot. Jack Nicklaus's long par-three sixteenth at Muirfield Village in his hometown of Columbus, Ohio, can be attacked only with a high, soft fade with a long iron—a shot on which Nicklaus the player developed the patent—and his severely divided greens on several courses in the 1980s emphasized tee-to-green play by making it very difficult to get up and down once a green had been missed. It seems safe to assume that Mackenzie and Perry Maxwell, the designers of severely contoured greens, were good chippers and putters; and that Albert W. Tillinghast, who declared during the building of Winged Foot Golf Club in New York that "the surest test of any man's golf is the approach to a closely guarded green," prided himself on his iron play.

NEARLY EVERY PRACTICING ARCHITECT HAS SERVED TIME AS an apprentice before hanging out his own shingle. Both Donald Ross and C. B. Macdonald, for example, learned golf-course design by spending time with the pioneer architect Old Tom Morris in St. Andrews during the 1890s—Ross as an assistant professional, Macdonald as a student at St. Andrews University. Dr. Mackenzie collaborated on his first efforts with the respected English designer Harry S. Colt. And contemporary designers Joe Lee, Bob von Hagge, and Tom Fazio can trace their fondness for sprawling, intricately shaped bunkers back through Dick Wilson and William Gordon, to Gordon and Wilson's mentor, William Flynn, who as construction superintendent at Merion in 1911 had spread white bedsheets where proposed bunkers might be so that designer Hugh Wilson could visualize the finished product. Ultimately, all golf architects' "family trees" spring from a seminal figure like Robert Bruce Harris or Desmond Muirhead, if not Old Tom Morris himself.

In the last thirty years, the profession has become very much a family business. Twenty designers practicing today are second- or third-generation golf architects, from Dan Maples, whose grandfather worked on construction crews with Donald

Ross, to Rees Jones and Robert Trent Jones, Jr.

It was the senior Trent Jones who developed golf architecture into the high-powered business we know now. Though Ross and Mackenzie were highly sought after in their time because of their reputation for building high-quality courses, it was Trent Jones who made the designer's "signature" a valuable commodity. A shrewd businessman, he recognized that modern developers were trying to sell housing lots or hotel space even before the course was completed, and cultivated such status that golfers would be attracted to a project on the force of his name alone. His trademark large and contoured greens were usually built well above the surrounding grade instead of subtly blended into it, making them easily recognizable. This greens style afforded plenty of opportunity to show off the flashed-sand bunkering that Trent Jones and Stanley Thompson had made an art form in the twenties.

Jones's successor at the pinnacle of the business was one

USGA Collection

Robert Trent Jones's revisions of Ross's Oakland Hills layout for the 1951 Open prompted eventual champion Ben Hogan (above, shown teeing off at the par-three seventeenth hole) to dub the course "the Monster."

For his work in toughening Open sites during the 1950s and 1960s, Trent Jones (right, with Sam Snead) earned the moniker of "Open Doctor."

Ron Whitten Collection

of the champions who had criticized his work—Jack Nicklaus. As a golfer, Nicklaus distinguished himself from others of his generation by his methodical and precise approach to the game. His approach to architecture was no different. His designs, starting with Muirfield Village, became celebrated for their fine visibility of target areas and hazards, high-quality construction, and immaculate, spare-no-expense maintenance. In contrast to many Tour professionals who lent their names to golf-course developments, Nicklaus insisted on approving every aspect of every one of his designs before the courses were seeded.

Nicklaus's method of operation, which made use of the latest technology—from computer graphics to faxed Polaroid photos, to keep the designer abreast of progress at his courses around the world—differed radically from that of his early mentor in the business, Pete Dye. Dye insisted that, no matter how good the plan, the finished product would be no better than the man who adapted it to the site and the earth. He prided himself on being a throwback to the early amateur architects, like George Crump of Pine Valley and Hugh Wilson of Merion, who spent every day nurturing their masterpieces.

Compared with the large companies of Nicklaus or Robert Trent Jones (which worked on a dozen or more courses at one time), Dye's business was very much a mom-and-pop operation. While Pete was spending most of his time watching the bulldozers and the shovels and rakes at work, his wife, Alice O'Neal, a gifted amateur player, ran much of the business end—handling phone calls, sorting out the best potential clients, and offering a second opinion on every phase of design, especially in regard to the placement of alternate forward tees for men and women. In recognition of her contributions, Alice Dye was belatedly elected the first female member of the American Society of Golf Course Architects in 1987.

Pete Dye designs often featured railroad-tie bulkheads, large "waste bunkers," and spectator mounds for tournament play. And his methods were decidedly unorthodox. At Harbour Town Golf Links in South Carolina, where Dye first collaborated with Nicklaus in 1969, one of Jack's contributions was to hit a bucket of balls with his nine-iron from the fifteenth fairway so Dye could draw a circle around the better ones to determine the size of the green. Dye refused to prepare detailed drawings of his designs, because he liked to change his mind as he watched a hole evolve during construction, and he didn't want clients to come back to him and complain that a hole wasn't being done according to plan. (A rare exception to his rule was the island-green seventeenth hole at PGA West in California, the final drawing of which was done on the back of a doorknob room-service order form from the La Quinta Hotel.) Indeed, Dye confided that some of his most original and popular designs were the result of construction screw-ups or misunderstandings, and he sometimes let his young shapers begin on a green site with little or no advance instruction,

Slim Aarons

Jack Nicklaus's architectural style, exemplified by the eighteenth at Castle Pines in Colorado, sharply delineates safety from trouble.

Among the marshes and pines of South Carolina's Low Country, architect Pete Dye fashioned one of his finest efforts, Harbour Town Golf Links on Hilton Head Island (above).

Dye takes the hands-on approach (right) during the routing and shaping of his courses.

Jim Moriarty

simply to give him something other than a blank canvas on which to design. This adaptability was a great asset in the modern era, when poor sites seldom suggested design ideas.

Golf-course architecture calls for inspiration. Herbert Fowler, the English designer of Walton Heath, surveyed his property from on horseback until, in a burst of creativity, he had his routing plan, leading Bernard Darwin to write, "I think his clients thought, quite unjustly, that he had not taken sufficient pains, because he could see so clearly and work so fast." Stanley Thompson, according to Trent Jones, did most of his designing at a drawing board in the company of "a bottle of Scotch and a good cigar." C. B. Macdonald confided that when he was stuck for ideas on contouring his greens, he would sprinkle some pebbles at random across a plan of the green and place the undulations according to their fall. And Alister Mackenzie liked to tell a yarn about a contractor who was praised for building greens with natural-looking undulations; when asked his secret, the contractor replied that he "simply employed the biggest fool in the village, and told him to make them flat."

WHILE GOLFERS AND CRITICS TODAY TEND TO BELIEVE THAT the modern method of design was invented by Trent Jones, Dye, and Nicklaus, a closer look at the past shows that things have not changed quite as much as it appears. It was

Ron Whitten Collection

Donald Ross, not Jones or Nicklaus, who first employed draftsmen and engineers to mass-produce his designs, way back in 1915; and it was Macdonald, not Dye, who first attempted to produce an artificial links course from swampland, at the Lido Golf Club on Long Island in 1917.

Today, as Ross explained in 1929, "the idea is to mold nature just sufficiently to give the greatest golf possibilities." Only the resources available to the architect and concern for the environment have changed what can be built. Today's architects are much more sensitive to ecological concerns than were their predecessors. To cite one example, whereas Dick Wilson's Doral Country Club was created thirty years ago by dredging and filling a swamp, totally obliterating the wetlands ecosystem, Pete Dye's Old Marsh Golf Club in south Florida installed an elaborate drainage network of plastic tile and artificial lagoons to recycle all its irrigation and run-off water and protect the surrounding marshes from the possibility of chemical or nitrate infiltration.

Meanwhile, golf architects have been constantly on the lookout for changes in the game itself, especially changes that might affect how all golf courses are played. Of special interest has been the liveliness of the golf ball. Architects from Nicklaus back to Donald Ross have worried that a newly developed "super ball" could make the game obsolete. The USGA listened, adopting dimensional standards for the modern golf ball in cooperation with the R&A in 1921. A 1930 advisory committee, chaired by architect/developer William Fownes of Oakmont, made additional recommendations. Further restrictions were adopted with the Initial Velocity Standard, set in 1942, and the Overall Distance Standard, adopted in 1976.

Ask any great golfer of the previous generation what has been the biggest change in the game, however, and he'll probably point to the improvement in course conditioning. The USGA has been at the forefront, founding its Green Section for turfgrass research and advisory services in 1920 under the auspices of Dr. C. V. Piper, at the United States Department of Agriculture. Today the Green Section has an operating budget of $2.5 million for providing its advisory service to courses across the United States, and an additional $1 million per year in researching improved turfgrass cultivars for use on courses.

The impact of turf research on golf courses and architecture has been enormous. Consider, for example, Donald Ross's masterpiece, Pinehurst No. 2. It had greens of oiled sand until the 1930s, when technology finally reached the point that good bermudagrass surfaces could be maintained. The technology of the 1980s permitted these same greens to be rebuilt to modern

Lido Golf Club on Long Island, a Charles Blair Macdonald creation, was sold during the Depression, but in its heyday, it was good enough to host qualifying for the 1925 Open. Here, a crowd follows Bobby Jones down the fairway.

The Bettmann Archive

At Pinehurst during the 1930s, the greenkeeping crew mows a swath (above).

In 1918 a worker sets out stolons—grass plant runners used to propagate new plants—on a green surface (top, right).

USGA agronomists (bottom, right) examine a test plot at Arlington Turf Farms in Virginia. The site is now occupied by the Pentagon.

Courtesy The Tufts Archives

USGA Collection

USGA Collection

specifications, their contours precisely replicated after computer mapping, and then resurfaced with a new cultivar of bentgrass bred specially to survive the heat of the Carolina sandhills.

Pete Dye, who served as a volunteer on the committee of the USGA Green Section before turning to golf architecture, credits much of his success to his use of different grasses to define the boundaries of the course. "What made Harbour Town such a success was the contrast in the grasses," says Dye. "Until Harbour Town, there had never been a course in the Carolinas with different grasses. The contrast in grasses has as much to do with the beauty of a course as the bunkers, the water, the rough, the trees."

The course superintendent must also be given his due. Indeed, most architects would agree that the golfer would prefer a poorly designed, well-maintained course than the reverse. Like the golf architect's, the superintendent's profession has evolved radically over the past hundred years, from making the best of natural conditions to relying on advances in science to maintain grass in hostile environments. This transformation is the result of the average golfer's never-ending desire for improved conditions, which he hopes will transform his game.

Unfortunately, though, the old-timers who remind us of all of the "improvements" in course conditioning have another

USGA Collection

point—that the standardization of playing conditions has robbed the game of much of the need for shotmaking skill and judgment of green speed, which were key elements not so long ago. For example, Mickey Wright points out that "in the fifties, every lie in a fairway would be different, where today it seems every lie is very, very good. And even from the fairways into the rough, which there seems to be very little of today compared to thirty, forty years ago, it just seems that, again, shotmaking ability is not a priority—that you can make the same swing, the same pass at the ball, no matter where you are, in the rough or in the fairway."

The most fundamental change in America has been the increasing reliance on aerial approaches to greens as opposed to the running shots frequently played on British links. Fairway irrigation, different varieties of grass, and improvements in clubs and balls all have conspired to make it easier for players to stop their approaches consistently, eliminating the uncertainty of the bounce in the running approach. The green chairman's and superintendent's goal of providing uniform playing conditions has also eliminated much of the "rub of the green" from the game. This was a matter of concern for architect H. S. Colt back in 1912. "When someone came up to me and admired the state of the green, out of sheer contrariness I objected, and said that the lies were getting much too good," he wrote. "What we want to do ... is to extract the very best golf from a man, and nothing does this so much as difficult lies and difficult stances."

Many believe that it is up to the golf architect to watch these changes in the game, and to respond in his designs so that change does not diminish the nature of the challenge which makes golf so captivating.

Max Behr put the responsibility elsewhere when he observed in *The American Golfer* in the 1920s, "Golf is a sport, not a game. The field of play is nature, a stationary, immovable opponent. Its extent is so great that it can neither be overcome, nor escaped. There is no necessity for artificial barriers. Play does not have to be systematically controlled. An opposite principle is involved. This principle is freedom. And by freedom we compel the golfer to control himself; that is to say, his instincts .... If he judges

Leonard Kamsler

Maintenance practices have come a long way since sheep kept the grass trim at Essex County Club in Manchester, Massachusetts (top, left).

By 1976 improved techniques and research helped Augusta National (above) become an emerald jewel for The Masters.

Rees Jones's Sandpines (above), a spectacular Oregon public course opened in 1993, received rave reviews from the moment the first ball was struck.

Dr. Alister Mackenzie (top, right), a camouflage expert during World War I, played a leading role in the Golden Age of golf architecture.

Aaron Chang

Bettmann/UPI

his skill is great enough, he will of his own accord go for a strategic hazard to gain an advantage just as the tennis player will go for the sidelines of the court."

This freedom is the essential appeal of golf and of the golf course. The object of the game is to get the ball in the hole in the fewest number of strokes, but there are no compulsory exercises along the way—we may do it with whatever shots we have mastered, or try others at the risk of failure. If we score efficiently, our method is beyond criticism. Furthermore, it is up to each golfer to measure success on his or her own terms.

More than this, the esthetic appeal of golf is in the freedom of the pursuit. The golf course is a beautiful landscape over which we roam freely. We can hit the ball anywhere we want, but we will have to go and extricate it from wherever we find it. This appeal is lost if the architect imposes his will excessively by placing so many hazards that the strategy becomes contrived, or so that the golfer has only one way to play the hole correctly. That is why the designer tries to minimize the penalties of water, jungle, or out of bounds; and why Dr. Mackenzie talked of eliminating the need to hunt for lost balls. Freedom of movement should not be inhibited.

In a country that celebrates freedom above all else, that is a very good reason golf will never lose its appeal.

1

The Recreational Player

Fat or thin, scratch or duffer, we have been somewhere together where nongolfers never go.—John Updike

Bobby Jones called it "the greatest game," but for millions of recreational golfers, it's simply a magnificent obsession. Once smitten, the golfer will go to any lengths to play the game. Grown men sleep in their cars to be first in line for early morning starting times. Golfers change jobs, move homes, abandon spouses just to play the game. The golf weekend, the golf vacation, the golf retirement—all are built around the sweet prospect of playing at every possible opportunity. Recreational golfers come in every size, every shape, every type. Some don the gear of their heroes—the plus fours, the technicolor shirts; others just throw on whatever they have at hand. Some golfers positively relish challenging the most extreme heat, the most searing cold, to chase the ball around the course. But every recreational golfer is drawn to the absorbing beauty of the game—the dewy mornings, the bracing autumn days, the scruffy nine that can be as much a cathedral to those who play it as Augusta National is to the giants of golf. They cherish the camaraderie of the

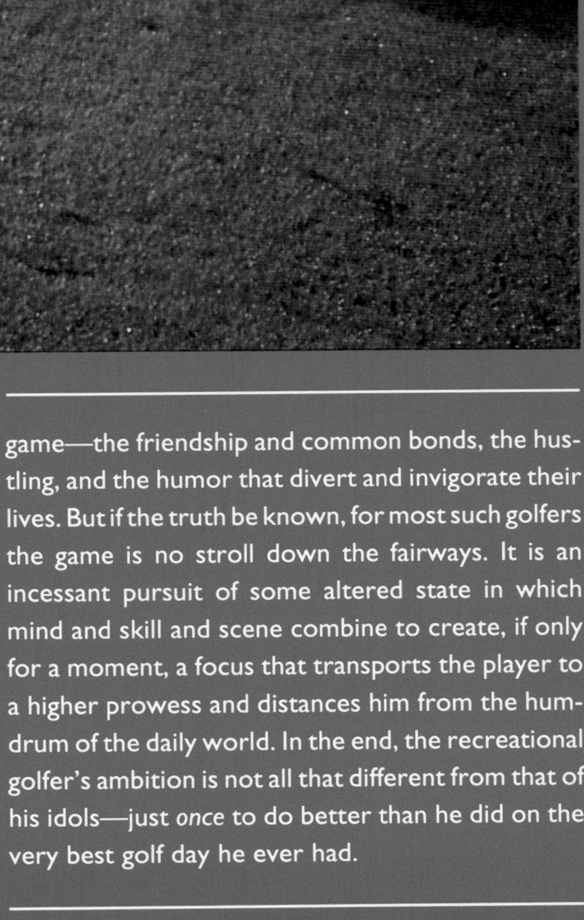

Brennon Jones

Wallner Collection/University of Louisville

2

Robert Gumpert

3

1 The tenth hole at Elmwood Country Club in White Plains, New York.
2 Off to the course: early golfers in Kentucky.
3 Studying the break, at the seventeenth green at Lincoln Park Golf Club in San Francisco.

game—the friendship and common bonds, the hustling, and the humor that divert and invigorate their lives. But if the truth be known, for most such golfers the game is no stroll down the fairways. It is an incessant pursuit of some altered state in which mind and skill and scene combine to create, if only for a moment, a focus that transports the player to a higher prowess and distances him from the humdrum of the daily world. In the end, the recreational golfer's ambition is not all that different from that of his idols—just *once* to do better than he did on the very best golf day he ever had.

Brennon Jones

4

Jeff Jacobson

5

David Liam Kyle

6

Leonard Kamsler

7

Jules Alexander

8

Eugene Richards

9

4 In the image of his heroes: a golfer at Elmwood Country Club.

5 Los Angeles inner-city kids get a chance to learn the game through the LPGA Junior Golf Program.

6 At Edwin Shaw Hospital Challenge Program's three-hole course in Akron, Ohio, the game is good therapy for neurological impairments.

7 Absorbed in his game: a pee wee in Coral Gables, Florida, 1969.

8 An after-school round at Westchester Country Club in New York.

9 A senior at the nine-hole Essex Golf Club in Iowa.

Andy Levin

10

Aaron Chang

11

Misha Erwitt

12

10 Lost in the rough at the Legends Moorland course in Myrtle Beach, South Carolina.

11 A golfer tracks her drive at Ala Wai Golf Course in Honolulu.

12 Putting on their spikes in the Shawnee Hills Golf Club parking lot in Cleveland.

Aaron Chang

13

Aaron Chang

14

Andy Levin

15

Brennon Jones

16

Jeff Jacobson

17

13 On the practice range at Ala Wai.
14 On the putting green at the same Hawaii course.
15 Challenging the cold at the Legends in Myrtle Beach.
16 A run for the green at Elmwood Country Club.
17 Eyeing the prize at the Los Angeles LPGA Junior Golf Program.
18 President Clinton (center) with Walt Patterson (left) and Paul Berry at Chenal Country Club in Little Rock, Arkansas.
19 In good form, a stroke victim at the Edwin Shaw Hospital Challenge Program course.
20 Lining up for starting times at Dyker Beach in Brooklyn, New York, 1960.

AP/Wide World Photos

18

David Liam Kyle

19

John Loengard/Life Magazine

20

Jeff Jacobson

21

USGA Collection

22

Amy Janello

23

24

Robert Gumpert

21 Putting practice at the LPGA Junior Golf Program in Los Angeles.
22 Surveying the course at Dorset Field Club in Vermont.
23 Leaving the first tee of the Green Course at Bethpage State Park.
24 A golfer strides toward the third hole at Lincoln Park Golf Club, close by Golden Gate Bridge.

Jay Maisel/Sports Illustrated

The Mental Challenge

David Noonan

Previous spread: He could have died out there, a doctor said, but Ken Venturi's almost superhuman effort to persist despite the hundred-degree heat at the 1964 Open at Congressional gave him the victory of his life.

It seemed Sam Snead was fated never to win the Open. In 1939 he reached the eighteenth hole of the last round at Philadelphia Country Club needing only a par five to win; he took an eight, finding two bunkers and three-putting the green (above).

Bettmann/UPI

When twenty-seven-year-old Sam Snead walked onto the eighteenth tee of the Philadelphia Country Club's Spring Mill Course in the final round of the 1939 United States Open championship, the tournament was his to win. A simple par five on the 558-yard hole would give him the title. But more than that, it would cap his swift and extraordinary rise to the top of the sport and establish him as golf s brightest star. After just three years on the professional circuit, the smooth-swinging Snead already had more than a dozen tour victories to his credit, including eight wins in 1938. It was clear to all who followed the game that the dapper young man from West Virginia was destined for greatness. An Open victory for Snead had seemed inevitable since his debut in the 1937 edition of the event, when he finished second, two strokes behind Ralph Guldahl. Now, finally, the moment was at hand; a par five would do it.

Snead made eight. He hooked his drive into the trampled rough, then took a brassie (a two-and-a-half wood) and knocked the ball into a bunker about 110 yards short of the green. Trying to get on in three, he played an eight-iron and left it in the bunker. He swung again and dumped the ball into yet another bunker just short of the green. He finally made it on in five, but he was still forty-five feet from the pin. He three-putted. In a matter of minutes, his great victory had become a horrifying defeat. "Sam Snead walked like one hypnotized through the stunned, muttering crowd," wrote Herbert Warren Wind. "He sat silently in the clubhouse trying to adjust himself to the unreal fact that he had taken an eight and blown the championship." Years later, Snead himself recounted the disaster in one of his books. He explained how he mistakenly thought he needed a birdie to win, and he confessed to the number-one sin in golf. "In all honesty," he wrote, "I have to admit that I was guilty of bad thinking."

With its subtle physics and even more subtle psychology, golf is the truest test of character in sports. It's a mind game in the purest sense of the words; the most formidable hazards a golfer faces in any given round are his own thoughts and emotions. If he is to control the flight of the ball, he must first control himself. That

Sam Snead, one of the greatest golfers of all time, could suffer such a calamitous reversal of form at such a critical moment graphically illustrates the fragile nature of the golf mentality. It couldn't have happened, but it did, as surely as you shanked that little pitch shot into that bunker not so long ago.

Disastrous collapses like Snead's are hardly rare. At least once a decade, it seems, some great champion on the verge of yet another triumph goes down in flames as the golfing public looks on in horror. In 1920 the legendary Harry Vardon had merely to play the last seven holes of the U.S. Open at five over par to win the title. He bogeyed them all and lost. In the 1966 edition of the same event, at Olympic in San Francisco, it was Arnold Palmer who disintegrated before our eyes, blowing a seven-stroke lead with nine holes to play in one of the most infamous breakdowns in the history of the game. "I don't know what happened to me yesterday," Palmer said the next day, after he had lost in the playoff to Billy Casper. "I guess it was a matter of timing." In fact, Palmer as much as admitted that he had started to think about breaking Ben Hogan's Open record of 276 as he made the turn in the final round. A one-over-par score of 36 on that last nine would have done it for him, so of course he shot 39 and ended up losing it all.

Now a sane person might ask: If people like Sam Snead and Arnold Palmer—*Snead and Palmer,* for God's sake—can fall apart so completely on a golf course, what hope is there for the rest of us, the so-called high-handicappers and the other mere mortals who venture out onto the verdant sward in pursuit of the little white ball? The answer, of course, is plenty. The stuff springs eternal, after all, and it does some of its springiest springing on golf courses. A feeling of hope, in fact, is very often the only thing that keeps me going on those too-frequent days when my swing has broken down and my head has exploded: hope that my next shot will be straight; hope that a four up ahead will balance the nine I just carded; hope that the beer will be cold at the halfway house. The truth is, grim golf phenomena like Palmer's self-immolation and, to cite a more recent example, Greg Norman's eerie string of losses via miracle shots by his opponents, don't intimidate average golfers; they fascinate them. Knowing that the game's best players are routinely tossed about by the same capricious winds that buffet him week in and week out is a comfort to Joe Bogey. It's not that he enjoys seeing others in pain, he's just relieved to know that his own pain is not unique.

For sure, the annals of the game are full of inspiring stories of golfers overcoming great obstacles to win championships. Witness Palmer's famous charge in the final round of the 1960 Open, when he birdied six of the first seven holes and went on to win after starting seven strokes back. Or Ken Venturi's stirring Open victory in 1964, when the format still called for thirty-six holes on the final day. Venturi shot a four-under-par 66 in the morning to pull within two of the lead. Then, after being warned

USGA Collection

Sometimes even the best fall apart under the pressure. Arnold Palmer had a seven-stroke lead over Billy Casper, coming into the final nine in the 1966 Open at the Olympic Club in San Francisco. Casper shot 32, but Palmer collapsed with a 39, and lost a playoff with Casper the next day.

Vicki Goetze tries not to lose her patience with her putter at the 1990 Girls' Junior at Manasquan, New Jersey. She went on to finish second to Sandrine Mendiburu.

by a doctor that he could *die of heat stroke* if he played the final round, Venturi went out and shot 70 to win by four strokes. And, hey, what about Billy Casper in 1966? Talk about never giving up. Bad as Palmer was, Casper still had to shoot 32 on the back nine to tie him in regulation, and then he had to come from two down with nine to go to win the playoff.

Such extraordinary victories are an exciting part of the game, and there are lessons to be learned from them. But it's during the catastrophic defeats that the complex psychodynamics that underlie the game are best glimpsed. Because, as every real golfer knows, golf isn't about winning; it's about trying to hold on to something that's very hard to hold on to, a fact of life neatly summed up by this quote from three-time U.S. Open champion Hale Irwin, which I overheard on the practice tee at a PGA tournament one day: "I haven't hit a ball for three weeks, so I don't know what I'm doing." He was exaggerating, of course, but he wasn't quite joking; his weary tone betrayed the hard grain of truth in the words.

GOLF IS THE EGO AND THE ID IN A PLAYOFF THAT NEVER ENDS. It's a solitary wandering in the manicured wilderness. It's man alone with his own mind. It's too much time to think and too much to think about. It's a dream and a nightmare. It's more like life than life itself. It's a game.

That's right. Golf is just a game. We have to remember that. George Archer, for one, has never forgotten that golf is a game, which may be one reason his friendly smile and easygoing demeanor are still intact after thirty years of big-time competitive golf. "It's a game," said Archer, the 1969 Masters champion and one of the most successful players on the Senior PGA Tour. "That's what's fascinating about it." Archer, who was hitting practice shots as he spoke, carefully studying the flight of each ball, seemed genuinely intrigued by the fact that he'd spent his entire adult life playing a game. "And I realize it's something I will never be able to play perfect," he continued. "But how good can I play it? *That's* the challenge of the game."

It is indeed, and the first step in meeting that challenge is understanding that golf is *not* just a game but a full-blown alternative universe, and when you are playing golf you are dwelling in that universe. As a matter of fact, it's not even you who dwells in that universe; it's your golf-self, the alternative version of you that emerges when you step onto a course. Your golf-self is basically the same you that your family and co-workers are familiar with, only funnier or nastier or noisier or quieter or angrier or happier or smarter or dumber or whatever. It's the essential you, the real you, and if you've played the game for any substantial period of time, you have most certainly been introduced. For the simple truth is there's no place to hide on a golf course, in spite of all the trees. As Arnold Haultain put it in 1908, in *The Mystery of Golf*: "Golf is a test, not so much of the muscle, or even of the brain and

Robert Gumpert

nerves of a man, as it is a test of his inmost veriest self; of his soul and spirit;—of his whole character and disposition . . .; of the entire content of his mental and moral nature as handed down to him by unnumbered multitudes of ancestors." Or, if you prefer a more recent take on the idea, there's this from a 1993 interview with Michael Murphy, author of *Golf in the Kingdom*: "I believe golf can be a doorway into the further reaches of the body and soul."

In the end, of course, the only thing the essential you wants to do is get the little ball down the fairway and in the hole and have fun doing it. That the successful pursuit of this seemingly pointless task would require an encounter with the deepest currents of one's being is the central irony of the game.

Naturally, it's the having-fun part that complicates matters; the fact that for most of us golf is a form of recreation, something we enjoy doing, something we want to enjoy doing, seems to me the real source of the mental challenge of the game. In my experience, there's a cruel conundrum at work: When I play well I have fun; when I have fun I play well; when I don't play well I don't have fun; when I don't have fun I don't play well. And it goes on like that, around and around, in a rhythm not unlike the slow turning of a three-wood in the air as it sails down the fairway after a bad shot.

To break the cycle, I have discovered, what the golfer must do is locate his true place in the golf universe. As a practical matter, what this usually comes down to is confronting and overcoming what I consider the single most insidious barrier to the enjoyment of the game of golf. I'm not talking about the swing—we'll wrestle that octopus in a moment—I'm talking about par.

What is this thing called par, anyway? According to the *USGA Rules of Golf*, par is "the score that an expert golfer would be expected to make for a given hole." Sounds harmless enough. What par really is, of course, is the completely unrealistic goal that virtually every golfer, regardless of handicap, sets for himself as he stands on the tee of "a given hole." Par is a pipe dream, a fantasy, a dangling carrot at the end of a 450-yard-long stick.

It's strange, really. Though it would never, ever occur to

Eugene Richards

An early morning golfer (top, left) at Lincoln Park in San Francisco.

Six players (above) search for the secret at Essex Golf Club in Iowa.

A Sunday outing at Van Cortlandt Park in the Bronx, New York. Edelmiro Mateo putts, while Francisco Santiago and Emilio Cerezo observe.

me that I might shoot par for a round of golf—I live in the mid-90s and the neighborhood suits me fine—every time I stick a tee in the ground the possibility of parring the hole I'm about to play crosses my mind. Which might not seem like such a big deal, except for the fact that *making par has absolutely nothing to do with my true place in the golf universe.* So for me to think about making par, even for a moment, is bad thinking. And we know where that leads—it leads to the land of quadruple bogeys and serial obscenities. And that's not golf. What I should do instead, what I *try* to do, is follow the sage advice of former USGA president H. H. Ramsay. "Every golfer should establish his own par on a hole and play for that par," Ramsay said in a 1934 article in *The American Golfer.* It was—it is—a revolutionary idea. It's simple and to the point, and not nearly as easy to put into action as you might think. After all, who wants to admit that double bogey is probably the best he can do on some holes? Not me, not you. But liberation from the tyranny of par is the key to finding your true place in the golf universe, and the price of that liberation is honesty, good old brutal honesty. So look yourself in the eye and accept yourself as the kind of golfer you actually are. Once you've done that, you can get down to the real heart of the matter—hitting the ball.

A ROUND OF GOLF IS ONE SWEET THING, A FLOWING RIVER OF movement out and around the course and back again. It is also a string of moments, complete unto themselves—the moments when the ball is in the air; the moments when you are walking down the fairway after it; the moments when you arrive at the ball and reacquaint yourself with it—hello ball; the moments when the ball disappears into the lake and you bid it farewell—good-bye ball. The critical moments, of course, are those just before you hit the ball—when you are standing over it, about to swing—and when you are actually swinging. It is those moments, taken all together, that define a round of golf and, ultimately, your life as a golfer. What defines those moments, obviously, are your thoughts and feelings as you live them. If they are the right thoughts and feelings, then bang, your swing will be true and the ball will probably go where you want it to go. If they are the other kind, you might never see that ball again. It's as simple and as complicated as that.

It's amazing, really, the variety of things that have flashed through my mind over the years while I was preparing to swing and when I was actually swinging a golf club. Besides the obvious technical thoughts about keeping my head down and my knees flexed and my left arm straight and my right elbow tucked in and my left heel down and all of that, I have, at one time or another, hit shots while balancing my checkbook, regretting having yelled at my children, imagining that my car was being stolen, planning dinner, remembering what autumn was like in the northeast when I was a boy, and worrying about my dog's flea problem. To make matters worse, I am also acutely sensitive to what's going on

Lee Janzen (above, on left) and Payne Stewart play the waiting game on the thirteenth tee at Baltusrol during the 1993 Open.

Though a three-time runner-up in the Women's Open, Nancy Lopez (top, right) has never managed to win the championship.

Andy Levin

Bob Straus

around me when I play golf— from the birds singing in the trees to the sirens screaming in the distance to the coins jingling in my partner's pocket.

The terrible truth is, I'm not unlike a lot of the golfers I caddied for when I was a kid—jittery characters with the nerves of rabbits and the swings of amphetamine abusers. I used to make a game out of distracting them at critical moments. On the greens, I wielded my shadow like a scalpel, letting it cut into the outermost edge of my high-strung victim's field of vision just as he was drawing his putter back. On the tees, the old accidental club-rattle at the top of the backswing was all it took to send yet another topped drive skidding down to the ladies' tee. And in the fairways, the trick was to start walking a fraction of a second too soon, while the jumpy son-of-a-gun was just coming into the ball. "I don't know, Mr. Shakes," I'd say, a concerned look on my young face, "that could be out-of-bounds. You'd better hit a provisional." It was cruel fun, I admit, but I am paying for it now; to wit, I think I heard a butterfly as I was preparing to tee off the other day. Which is impossible, I know (I hope), but such are the workings of my golfing mind, a teeming snakepit of neuroses, tics, and distracting thoughts.

At least I don't have the yips. Not yet, anyway. I've read about Ben Hogan's battle with the eerie affliction in his later years, and I don't think I could handle it. "I apologize to everyone for taking so long to putt," he once said during a tournament. "I still freeze some, but I'm trying. I can hear people in the gallery saying, 'Why doesn't that man go ahead and putt?' I wish I knew the answer." Hogan somehow managed to retain his sense of humor in spite of the yips, and according to Herbert Warren Wind, he even came up with a solution for the disorder. "Lamenting his lapses one afternoon," Wind wrote, "[Hogan] announced ruefully that he would not be averse if, instead of having to putt out, golfers simply fired their approaches or their chips into enormous funnels positioned over the target. 'You'd just sock the ball into the funnel on, say, the seventh, and it would roll out of a pipe at the other end and onto the eight tee.' " Sounds good, but I suspect that socking it into the funnel wouldn't be nearly as easy as Hogan suggested. I suspect, in fact, that the funnels would become just

Doctors said that Ben Hogan would never walk after his 1949 car accident. A year later, he won the Open in a playoff at Merion (above).

At the 1964 Masters, South African Gary Player (top, right) lines up a putt on the eighteenth green. Longtime rival Arnold Palmer would win, with a 276 total.

AP/Wide World Photos

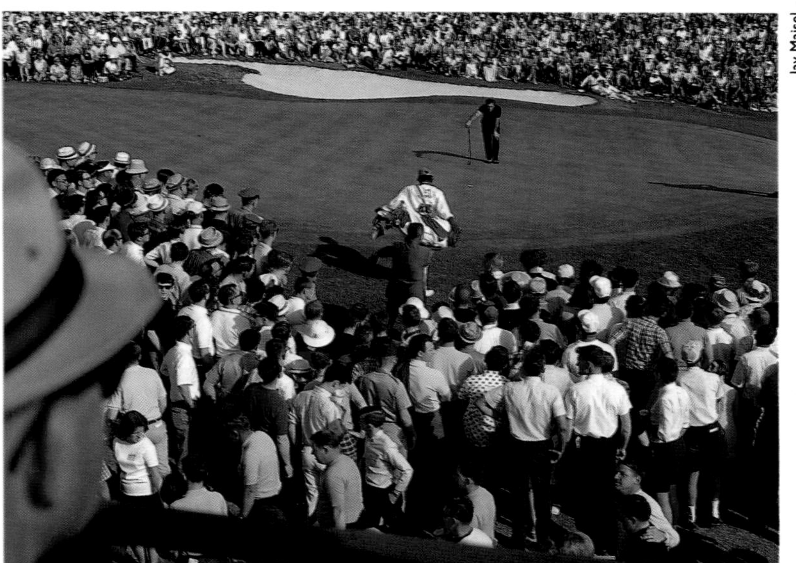

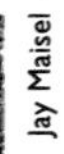

Jay Maisel

one more thing for me to worry about. I mean, exactly how wide would the funnels be, anyway?

What I need to do when I play golf is take all my extraneous thoughts and "leave them in the van," as Jackie Steinmann, the coach of the women's golf team at the University of California at Los Angeles, would say. That's what Steinmann tells her golfers to do when they are on their way to play in a tournament. "Take the exams, the term papers, the dates, the parties, all the things you're worrying about," she instructs them, "dump them into an imaginary bag and leave the bag in the van when you get to the course. Forget about everything for the next few hours and just play golf."

Steinmann, a member of the National Golf Coaches Association Hall of Fame and LPGA Coach of the Year in 1988, has been coaching at UCLA since 1977. Her team won the NCAA championship in 1991. Since most of her players also work with personal swing coaches, Steinmann can devote much of her time to the mental side of the game, helping her team members develop a winning attitude about their golf and about themselves. She places heavy emphasis on goal-setting, positive thinking, and positive reinforcement and uses a variety of techniques to get her message across. Her players not only write out and sign a list of personal goals for the season; they sign other documents as well, including one that says "I accept my swing."

Many of the techniques Steinmann uses were originally developed by Chuck Hogan of Sports Enhancement Associates of Sedona, Arizona. Hogan, a PGA-certified teaching pro, is a new-style golf teacher who takes instruction well beyond swing mechanics. Golf was not meant for the constant consumption and processing of facts about the swing, Hogan writes in his book *Learning Golf.* "It was meant for the freedom of mind and body to bond with an environment in which the game can be fully *played.*" One among a flock of golf gurus who have emerged in the last decade or so, Chuck Hogan has worked with touring pros John Cook, Peter Jacobsen, and Duffy Waldorf, among others. Hogan loves the game of golf but hates the way it is presented and taught.

Robert Gumpert

Richard Dole

Lincoln Park pro Tom McCray (left) shows the hip turn to fellow San Franciscan Pat Mulligan; Nick Faldo (above, on left) focuses on his guru, David Leadbetter, for a quick practice-tee fix; and 1925 Open champion Willie Macfarlane (below) ensures that 1924 All-America quarter-back Harry Stuhldreher uses his legs correctly on the backswing.

The Bettmann Archive

"Just look around at the explosion of golf instruction books, videos, and magazines," Hogan notes. "There are heaps and gobs of material on what to do when you swing, or what to do during any portion of the swing, regardless of how minuscule that portion may be!" He sees the booming interest in the mental side of the game as a reaction against this tidal wave of technical information.

Above all, Hogan wants to demystify golf and take the anxiety out of it for the average golfer. In a chapter called "What Is Golf?" he offers this radical advice: "When you play golf, just play golf. Here's you, here's the ball, there's the target. Go to it. Hit the ball to the target as best you can. Find the ball and do it again. Experience, adjust, experience, adjust . . . . The golf course is made for playing a game! So go there and *play* golf."

A lot of what Hogan says makes sense—especially on the subject of relaxing and having fun with the game—but I can't say I agree with all of his ideas. There is this, for instance, from a chapter titled "There Is No Such Thing As Failure": "Golf is playing. In play there is no such thing as failure. When you make a swing, hit a ball, or stroke a putt, there will be an outcome to your energy. Something will happen. The result of your experience is just that—a result. Don't let yourself or others define the result in labels like 'bad' or 'failure.' "

I don't know, maybe it's the Irish Catholic in me, but to call that tee shot I sliced out onto the freeway a while back

Father knows best: Francis Ouimet teaches daughters Janice and Barbara how to address the ball.

The Bettmann Archive

(Interstate 5, seventh hole, Wilson Golf Course, Griffith Park, Los Angeles) anything but "bad," not to mention "ugly," would be an abuse of the English language and just plain wrong, as any number of surprised motorists would surely agree.

All the great golfers of the century, from Francis Ouimet to Tom Watson, have written about the mental side of the game, and there is one thing they all agree on: the game must be played "one shot at a time." If there is a single commandment that must be obeyed to play good golf, that's it. It's a cliché of course, a hoary bit of advice that ranks right up there with "keep your head down" in the pantheon of hackneyed tips. But the truth is, it's the truth. The great Mickey Wright put it best: "The old trite saying of 'one shot at a time,' it wasn't trite to me. I lived it." It's remarkable, really, the way golf, this complex game, can be boiled down to its basic unit—the individual shot. Though there is an infinite variety of shots and circumstances under which they must be made, in the end each shot makes the identical demand on the golfer: total concentration.

"Emotional control is something I had to work on just as much as I did the golf swing when I went out on tour," Betsy Rawls once explained. "Anger, self-pity, fear of course. All those emotions have to be fought against all the time. Of course, pressure is nothing more than just fear: fear of making a mistake, fear of missing a putt, fear of looking foolish. And that's why those short putts to win tournaments are so difficult, because people project how bad they're going to feel if they miss it, or what people are going to think of them if they miss it. And so all of that has to be overcome. You overcome it best by concentrating on something positive. And you can't just *will* fear away. To overcome that fear you have to concentrate so hard on what you're trying to do that you block out the fear."

In a famous 1924 article titled "The Eight-Inch Golf Course," Eddie Loos described the "proper mental patterns" the golfer must develop to gain a reliable swing, likening them to dress patterns and architectural blueprints. There was a stance pattern, a grip pattern, and so on. He compared playing golf to reciting poetry: "If you wanted to learn a verse—wanted to learn to speak it effectively—you would commit it to memory, with every inflection and emphasis necessary to make a good delivery. This would be your 'pattern.' And—when you wanted to deliver the verse—mentally you'd fish out your pattern and go ahead—practically the same every time, gaining skill, ease, and certainty with repetition. It is exactly the same thing with the game of golf—every shot, successful or otherwise, is the result of a mental pattern."

The problem is, fishing out your mental swing patterns—focusing on the myriad details of the swing itself—is the surest way to blow a shot; taking a mental inventory of your body parts as you prepare to strike the ball is like reviewing a schematic drawing of your car before you hit the brakes in an emergency.

Simon Bruty/Allsport

Likewise, any thoughts about the consequences of the shot, good or bad, are likely to distract you from the proper execution of your swing. As every golfer knows, thinking about shanking that simple little nine-iron into a pond greatly increases the odds of doing exactly that.

So if you don't want to think about how you are going to hit the ball, and you don't want to think about what's going to happen to the ball when you do hit it, what's left? Actually, according to Bobby Jones and Ben Hogan, the thing to do is pick out parts of the swing to think about and then only think about them for part of the swing, or something like that.

"As a matter of fact, I do not believe it possible to play a proper shot while thinking of more than three parts of the motion of the stroke," Jones wrote in 1930. "But unfortunately for the peace of the world, the three things alter themselves from time to time; some that worry us now, by constant practice become habits and are replaced by others equally harassing." At the time, Jones's three things were "first, an unhurried, smooth, and amply long backswing; second, a generous break of the wrists at the top of the swing; and third, a firm downward punch with the left arm through the ball."

John Iacono/Sports Illustrated

Jack Nicklaus (top, left) thinks majors are easier to win, even though the competitors are plentiful, because only a handful of the players have the mental toughness and confidence to contend for golf's greatest titles.

Power hitter and 1991 PGA champion John Daly, who would go on to finish third, wedges out of what looks like a tight spot at the 1993 Masters (above).

For his part, Hogan implied in his book *Five Lessons* that he got all of his thinking out of the way during the first half of the swing. "After you have initiated the downswing with the hips," he wrote, "you want to think of only one thing: hitting the ball."

Then there is the advice Michael Murphy received from his mystical golf teacher, Shivas Irons, during the fateful round of golf at the center of *Golf in the Kingdom*: "Ye try too hard and ye think too much. Why don't ye go wi' yer pretty swing? Let the nothingness into yer shots." Following that mysterious tip, Murphy achieves the breakthrough that fans of the book live to recreate: "I became more and more aware of the *feeling* of the game, of how it was to walk from shot to shot, how it was to feel the energy gathering as I addressed the ball, how the golf links smelled. It was a new way to play for me; I had always been so focused on the score and the mechanics of my swing."

In the end, all golfers are after the same thing—those sweet and elusive moments when all the pieces finally come together and they find themselves playing that cool, quiet golf, that game within the game we all know exists, the one we know we can get to if we can just stop wanting it long enough to let it happen.

Twenty-year-old Mia Loejdahl has been playing golf for fifteen years. A member of the UCLA women's golf team, she hits

Courtesy Winged Foot Golf Club

Standing on the eighteenth tee at Winged Foot West in the final round of the 1929 Open, Bobby Jones knew he needed par to force a playoff with Al Espinosa. He got it, and the next day won the title.

Brennon Jones

the kind of crisp iron shots I look forward to hitting in my next life, and she speaks with the easy self-confidence of the naturally talented athlete. Asked what it feels like when she's playing her best golf, she answered without hesitation. "There's this harmony," she said, her voice light with guileless enthusiasm. "Everything is just so easy. You're over your putt and you know it's going in. You just know it."

Dwelling in another part of the golf universe is Madison Mason, a twenty-handicapper who flirted with the game for twenty years before getting serious about it in his forties. Like most average golfers, he "gets it going" every now and then and plays solid, consistent golf. It might last for a few shots or a few holes or even an entire round; he never knows. He only knows it won't last too long. "It's such a tenuous, ephemeral thing," he said, describing the feeling. "It's like this time when I was a kid, I had this hummingbird in my hands, and I wanted to take it home and show it to my mother." He cupped his hands in front of him. "It was such a delicate thing, you know, walking home with that hummingbird. I'll never forget it. It was vibrating, and I had to vibrate with it. I had to walk just right—not too fast, not too slow—or it would have just flown away." He opened his hands; the long-ago hummingbird flew away. "That's what good golf is like."

My own golf satori, the closest I have come to mastering the mental challenge of the game, lasted a brief nine holes, but I remember it well. It was part Bobby Jones, part Ben Hogan, and part Shivas Irons, triggered by a Gene Littler tip I read somewhere about slowing down the start of the backswing. I played the first nine holes of the round in my usual blurry way, talking too much and concentrating too little. Then, on the backside, it kicked in. Each time I stepped up on the tee, I zeroed in on the head of my driver, my trusty old black Haig Ultra. And somehow, for some reason, I got it. Suddenly I was there, the ball was there, and the club was there. It was just the three of us, and we all knew exactly what to do. And that's the only thing I remember, besides my score, which was my lowest ever for nine holes. When I think about that round, the only thing I see is the head of that club moving oh so slowly away from the ball. The swing was slow and

Robert Gumpert

Out of the chute: at the fourth hole of Long Island's Bethpage Black Course, a top municipal track (top, left).

Oblivious to the setting, this San Francisco public golfer (above) only has eyes for his shot.

Tom Kite holds the lead on Sunday as he leaves the first tee during the 1989 Open at Oak Hill in Rochester, New York. It was not to be, though; a poor round left him five strokes behind the eventual winner, Curtis Strange.

Robert Walker

easy, the drives were straight and true. I didn't think about anything else, and I don't remember anything else.

Almost better than experiencing mental mastery was meeting it in person and talking to it. It was the day before the start of the 1993 Los Angeles Open. I watched Tom Kite on the practice tee for two hours. His concentration was total; each ball was hit with purpose. In the three years since he had turned forty, Kite had won five times on the tour, including the 1992 U.S. Open. He was playing the best golf of his life at a time when, according to conventional wisdom, his game should have been eroding. I caught him as he headed for the putting green and asked him how that could be. "I think better," was his instant reply. I followed him through the crowd. He signed autographs as he walked. There was an aura about him, the unmistakable air of a winner. We talked as he putted. "Nobody thinks the way they should on every single shot," he said, "nobody's that good. You were born human." He described his mental approach as "effective thinking."

"You do whatever is necessary that allows you to hit good shots," he said. "Sometimes that might be telling yourself the truth, sometimes that might mean tricking yourself." But without a doubt, he emphasized, the most critical factor was the elimination of negative thoughts: "Every time you have a negative thought or a bad thought gets in your mind, catch it as fast as you can and change it." He bent over another putt and eyed the hole. What does he see, I wondered, that I don't see? I wanted to know more and started a long and complicated question.

Suddenly he stopped putting and looked right at me. "It's not really important to know about it," he said enigmatically, "as long as you do it." More mystery. "Is it instinct," I asked as he went back to his putting, "or is it something you learn?" He turned on me, eyes burning, impatient with my prying. "Don't try to make it black and white," he said. "You try to make it black and white, you're missing the whole point."

Four days later, when Tom Kite came from four strokes back with seven holes to play to win the tournament, I got the point.

The Bettmann Archive

The Business of Golf

Peter Andrews

Previous spread: It's a Pinehurst golf holiday for these players, who have come by bus from Wilkes-Barre, Pennsylvania. Among the golfers are a doctor, a city commissioner, a dentist, a cashier, a realtor, an attorney, a broker, and a judge.

His 1993 Masters victory meant more to Bernhard Langer (above, being congratulated by runner-up Chip Beck) than just prize money and a green jacket. Endorsements and other financial opportunities were his for the taking.

Stephen Szurlej/Golf World

When Bernhard Langer held his arms together as if in great pain to stroke home the final putt of the 1993 Masters, he did more than win a check for $306,000 and a green jacket that he is not permitted to wear off the grounds of the Augusta National Golf Club. He set in motion a business machine that will, in all likelihood, earn him at least $2 million by the time the last Deutschemark flutters into his bank account.

This assumes Langer is properly managed, and since he is a client of the mammoth International Management Group, the chances are he is. The name of this particular game is "endorsements," and no one plays it more skillfully than IMG. It is difficult to assign a specific dollar value to the winning of an individual tournament. Langer, who had also won The Masters in 1985, was already earning $3 million a year for endorsing such varied items as Adidas shoes, the American Express card, Hugo Boss clothing, Ebel watches, Lufthansa Airlines, Mercedes-Benz, and Wilson Sporting Goods. Naturally, all of Langer's clients will be reminded of how good he looked on television with his golden hair and his new baby held in a homey embrace by Jackson Stephens, the reclusive president of Augusta. And then perhaps there will be a new company eager to associate itself with Germany's Master of the Green. It will be another $2 million easy and soon and just for starters.

The merchandising of a golf champion is a complicated business in which golf skill is only one consideration. Scott Simpson, who outdueled Tom Watson to win the U.S. Open in 1987, has a solid swing and quiet personality. He is a decent, honorable man. Unhappily, he is not, by Madison Avenue standards, a particularly interesting one. Simpson profited by his victory through such mundane things as golf-equipment endorsements, which were all very pleasant. But Simpson's haul was no match for the golden harvest that Greg Norman, once described as looking like the man you hire to assassinate James Bond, had reaped the year before by winning the British Open. In short order IMG had Norman's name inked to $12 million worth of

Bob Straus

Bob Libby

endorsement contracts. For $3 million he would act as a spokesman for Qantas Airlines and Hertz rental cars. For another $3 million he would be the front man for a Japanese-owned real-estate development going up in his native Australia. Reebok paid Norman $2 million for the right to sew his signature into a line of sports clothes. Then there were minor matters such as $500,000 to endorse Epson computers and $1.5 million to drink and sing the praises of a pair of Australian beers, Swan Lager and Castlemaine XXXX, two things he was already doing anyway. This torrent of cash, because IMG understands such matters, was routed through a Dutch company to minimize income taxes.

For a golfer so full of bright promise, Norman went on to a curious career in which spectacular wins were punctuated by unexpected, heartbreaking losses. Four times he was looking at a putt on the eighteenth hole to win when an opponent holed out from off the green to beat him. However, he bore these reversals with such good cheer that he cemented himself in the affections of the golfing public, which understands the quixotic nature of the game, more firmly than if he had won. As a result, in 1993 Norman was still being rewarded with endorsement contracts of $7 million a year. Indeed, his success has been so great that the next year he hired away IMG's man in Melbourne, Australia,

Fred Vuich/Allsport

Greg Norman's rugged looks (top, left)—and a 1986 British Open—brought him $12 million in contracts in the 1980s.

For Patty Sheehan, as with most touring pros, a bag is a billboard too (bottom, left).

Even at events limiting corporate ads, like Jack Nicklaus's Memorial in Ohio (above), you can't miss manufacturer logos.

The Bettmann Archive

Frank Williams, and struck out on his own. You have to be as big as Jack Nicklaus to do that sort of thing.

The undisputed King of Golf Endorsements, of course, is Arnold Palmer, as he has been for more than three decades. Palmer's annual haul is valued at $10 million.

Winning even a single major championship can provide the golfer with an extended shelf life. In the manner of a Member of the Victorian Order, who can forever affix MVO after his name, the winner will always be identified as such. Bill Rogers, who won the British Open in 1981, was still collecting residual endorsement money from Japan for his efforts a dozen years later.

And now for one of those illuminating comparative statistics without which no business account would be complete. In 1945, before there was an IMG, Byron Nelson, a moon-faced Texan with the swing of a metronome, shot something like 320 under par for the season on his way to winning nineteen tournaments, eleven of them in succession. It remains the most stunning achievement in the history of professional golf. Nelson looked around for some financial compensation and was eventually rewarded with a check for $200 for the rights to put a drawing of his face on a box of Wheaties.

Bettmann/UPI

Taking home the prize money: Gene Littler (top) at the Tournament of Champions in Las Vegas in the mid-1950s; Byron Nelson (above) at the Belmont Country Club Open in Massachusetts; and Arnold Palmer (right) at the 1957 Houston Open.

The Bettmann Archive

These players at Ala Wai Golf Course in Honolulu, and 24 million fellow golfers, fuel a $30-billion-a-year industry.

Aaron Chang

As Louise Suggs, hard-hitting U.S. Women's Open champion in 1949, noted when comparing her record of fifty LPGA Tour victories for $200,000 in purse money with Pat Bradley's thirty victories for $4.5 million, "They say everything is relative. Well, it sure as hell ain't that relative."

The stratospheric income of a successful professional golfer is only the most immediately dramatic element of the current swank American golf scene. Touring professional Peter Jacobsen once said, "Golf professionals are like bears in the zoo. We may be fun to watch, but we aren't the game. The game is the millions of people who come out every day and play golf because they love it."

When considered as part of the overall American golf industry, touring professionals, for all their inflated pay checks, are selling jams and jellies from a card table by the side of the road. The National Golf Foundation, which keeps track of such things, estimates that Americans spend approximately $30 billion a year on the game. This includes expenditures for green fees at public facilities and resorts, private club memberships, equipment and apparel, golf travel, and buying homes connected with golf-course developments. Considering that roughly 24 million Americans over the age of twelve played 500 million rounds last year, that comes to an average cost of $60 per round. As a statistical proposition, the figure may seem to have the numerical significance of adding up all the telephone numbers in America and dividing by everybody listed in the phone book to arrive at the average American telephone number. In fact, it represents something close to the typical cost of a round at a high-level private facility. It may be pleasant to think that between the hacker who pays $5 to play on a hardscrabble municipal layout and Las Vegas mogul Steve Wynn, who ponied up a reported $35 million to build his own private course, American golfers are, on average, playing at rather nice clubs.

Who pays this kind of money to play golf? The 24-million figure stated earlier is only marginally useful. The NGF, for its purposes, calculates that anyone over the age of twelve who played so much as a single round in a given year is a golfer. The golf industry uses a different set of statistics in determining the extent of its potential market.

As with all numbers involved in an industry as fragmented as golf, these figures are a little slippery, but they will serve as reasonably accurate benchmarks. That 24 million breaks roughly in half between "recreational" golfers, who play between one and seven rounds a year, and "core" golfers, who play eight rounds or more. The core group breaks in half again into serious golfers and fanatics. There is a rough calculation in the industry that twenty percent of all golfers play eighty percent of the rounds and buy eighty percent of the equipment. These are the golfers about whom regular people make jokes. They are the ones who roll into the parking lot of the Papago Municipal Golf Course in Phoenix

Courtesy Ralph W. Miller Golf Library/Museum

at 2:30 in the morning to be in line when the gates open at 5:45 to get a ticket they can exchange for a tee time when the golf shop opens forty-five minutes later. They are the ones who play in weather that would keep the Coast Guard in port. They are the spiritual descendants of the golfer who stopped putting just long enough to put a hand over his heart when the cortege bearing his spouse passed on the way to the cemetery. They are the game.

Although it may be hard to believe today, one of the appeals of golf when it developed in Scotland more than five hundred years ago was that it was cheap. You didn't have to pay an architect to lay out a golf course when sheep would place your bunkers for you just by lying down to stay out of the wind. Clubs were literally that: You could whittle your own from a stray branch. And as for the golf ball, a top hat full of feathers that were boiled and then stuffed into a leather casing got you started nicely. It took a full day to make four good featheries, but they lasted a long time.

By the time golf came to America, it was swathed in gentility. In 1886 the *Tribune Book of Open-Air Sports* called the game "a pleasing compromise between the tediousness of croquet and the hurly burly of lawn tennis." An 1895 journalist was pleased to call golf "a game of good society," while *Outing Magazine* expressed the hope that golf, along with tennis, yachting, and polo, would not "offer any attractions to the more vulgar elements."

This conjures an elegant if somewhat stiff picture of well-dressed gentlemen and ladies spending a pleasant summer's day biffing away at a ball that was only infrequently hit out of sight. Such a rustic idyll could not last forever, however. Bernard Darwin, the father of all golf writers, once remarked, "Men will do anything in reason to add a cubit to their stature as drivers," and in proof of that we live today in the Age of Paraphernalia. The feathery, which held sway for four hundred years, yielded in the mid-nineteenth century to the gutta-percha, a cheaper and more durable ball that was molded from sap drawn from trees grown in India. One of the first promotion tours in the history of golf took

Bill Anderson Collection

New balls move down the assembly line at a Spalding plant in 1947 (top, left).

Even as early as the turn of the century, golf figured in vacation plans. The course and hotel at Poland Springs, Maine (above), drew holiday-minded players from the Northeast.

Robert Walker

The annual PGA Merchandise Show (left) in Orlando is the golf industry's extravaganza; thousands of merchandisers display their wares to the country's club professionals.

The register keeps ringing at pro shops like that at Lew Galbraith Golf Course in Oakland (top, right).

Terence Miskell, a contestant at the 1990 Amateur Public Links, gets help from the Eastmoreland Country Club gallery in his search for a stray shot (bottom, right). His ball is just one of 200 million lost each year, a boon to the manufacturers.

place in 1900 when Harry Vardon, the then three-time winner of the British Open who helped establish the modern game, came to America to promote a gutta-percha ball named in his honor, the "Vardon Flyer." Although the tour was a great personal success for Vardon, who pocketed several thousand dollars playing exhibition matches, his ball was a flop.

It was done in by the golf ball that is essentially the ball with which we are familiar. It was the wondrous creation of a Cleveland golfer named Coburn Haskell. Haskell was a keen, if only moderately skilled, golfer who found the gutta-percha to be a cumbersome affair. One day in 1898 while visiting the Goodrich Rubber Company, he got the idea of making a golf ball by wrapping a rubber core with elastic bands. By 1903 balls were encased in balata; five years after that, they were given their distinctive dimpled cover. Known as "Bounding Billies," the new rubber-cored balls captured the Olympic Games ideal of higher, farther, faster, and put twenty yards on everybody's drive. If the rubber-cored ball did not putt as well as the gutta-percha, it got to the green sooner, and that was good enough for most golfers.

Golf is a mysterious calling in which players are ruled more by their senses than by their intelligence. When we strike a golf ball, we are all certain it flies better if, at impact, it makes a sound that goes "click" rather than "clack." It is no more useful to tell a golfer that a ball is an inanimate object that does not know what sound it makes than it is to explain to a wary child that a monster is not living under the bed. We know better. And a mighty industry has grown up to provide us with balls that make that comforting sound.

In 1992 American manufacturers sold approximately 24 million dozen "top-grade" golf balls. Top-grade, according to industry standards, indicates balls that retail for at least $11 a dozen. We will relegate 5 million dozen or so that sell for less to driving ranges, to the dustbin of industry calculation, and ignore them. Even so, we have a chilling statistic. In the last five years, Americans bought more than 1.4 billion top-grade golf balls. Where did they go? Apart from the odd globe that figured in a hole-in-one and is now preserved on the mantelpiece or the

Victoria Rouse

Ron MacPike

relatively few remanded to the shag bag, there is no particular reason to keep a golf ball. Since the modern ball is likely to be lost before it can be cut, it is reasonable to assume that in the last five years Americans have collectively lost more than 1 billion balls. And yet, golfers keep coming back for more. Surely no other sporting endeavor can match that kind of dogged perseverance in the face of such manifest futility.

Before we proceed, a word of appreciation concerning the golf ball is in order. In these days when complaining about how expensive everything has become amounts to a litany, the golf ball is a triumph of American ingenuity. In 1960 a sleeve of three high-quality golf balls cost $3.75. Since then the Consumer Price Index has more than quadrupled, which means that same sleeve should fetch around $16. Instead, it sells for about $8.50. Increased volume and vigorous competition have kept prices down. And thanks to the miracle of a Surlyn cover, we now pay, relative to inflation, about half as much for a ball we can't cut as we did for one we could.

Then there is the equipment needed to send the ball wherever it is going. In 1992 Americans spent approximately $885 million to purchase 12 million new golf clubs of all kinds, from the putter to the driver. That comes to roughly $73.75 a club, which is a lot when you figure you can have as many as fourteen

Golf served as a morale booster at this Los Angeles Times*-sponsored defense industry tournament, held in 1943 at Inglewood Links in California.*

Whittington Collection/USC Library

in your bag at any one time. The market in used clubs is enormous but beyond calculation for this essay.

The relationship between golfers and their equipment is highly personal. Arnold Palmer has used more than 2,000 drivers without ever quite finding the one that was exactly right for him. Sam Snead, on the other hand, played with the same driver for more than twenty-five years, until the steel soleplate was worn as thin as a razor blade from sweeping the grass more than a million times. When the persimmon head of his driver finally broke apart, Snead said he cried "like a hurt wolf." He glued the pieces of his driver back together and returned to the course to play with it some more.

There is frequently an element of faddishness in golf equipment, as players rush to the pro shop rather than the practice tee to solve their golfing problems. The master innovator and merchandiser in these matters is Karsten Solheim, a onetime cobbler who taught himself engineering well enough to design Ping irons, the best-selling clubs in golfing history. So successful were Solheim's creations that he is now included in the *Forbes* magazine roster of the four hundred richest people in America. Although the list contains many accomplished golfers, Solheim, a shaky twenty-handicapper, is the only one who got there entirely by his income from golf.

For a while, wedges held everyone's attention. To the pitching wedge and sand wedge were added the Lob Wedge, the Finesse Wedge, and other clubs of varying degrees of loft until a golfer who carried fewer than three was made to feel underequipped. The most recent craze is the oversized driver. Big-headed drivers had been around for a long time, but were never promoted with the marketing skill of Ely Callaway, a former textile tycoon who went into the golf-club business at a time when most executives are nearing mandatory retirement age. He took an enlarged stainless steel clubface and gave it a sweet spot big enough for a croquet mallet. Then, to give it some oomph, he named it Big Bertha, after the huge World War I siege gun, and put it on the market. Callaway's revenues doubled for four consecutive years, and he moved up to become one of the top-ten clubmakers worldwide.

While the equipment business continues to be brisk, there is a sobering thought for the consumer. Evaluations at the USGA research and test center in Far Hills, New Jersey, indicate that an equipment change, almost any equipment change, can improve a golfer's performance for a time. Without proper instruction, however, such improvement will not last.

Golf instruction has become a good business as well. What was once the exclusive province of the individual professional standing on the practice tee and being paid by the half-hour for counsel and advice has now gone corporate. *Golf Digest*, devoted primarily to instruction, is the largest single-interest publication in the United States. Additionally, *Golf Digest* operates a series of golf

Stephen Szurlej/Golf Digest

Stephen Szurlej/Golf World

Payne Stewart (left), striding up the eighteenth at Hazeltine National in Minnesota to take the 1991 Open title, wears an outfit that proclaims his sponsor: the National Football League.

ABC's Brent Musburger (above) catches 1993 Open champion Lee Janzen and wife Beverly in the first flush of victory. More than 1,600 journalists covered the Baltusrol event.

schools at which students pay as much as $3,000 a week to stay at fashionable resorts such as The Cloister in Sea Island, Georgia, to work on their games. Arnold Palmer and Jack Nicklaus have recently opened their own golf schools. David Leadbetter, guru to such professionals as Nick Faldo, normally charges $300 an hour, which is more expensive than a Park Avenue psychiatrist who has to provide his own couch and Kleenex. Under the direction of IMG, Leadbetter has franchised his method of instruction from here to Thailand. A second sobering thought: Without proper practice, instruction won't help much either.

There have been two discernible economic booms in the American golf industry within this century. The first came during the Roaring Twenties, when just about anybody could make money and Robert Tyre Jones, Jr., was the beau ideal of sport. The second was ushered in during the 1950s, when golf discovered television and President Dwight Eisenhower, who together set the stage for Arnold Palmer to electrify a new generation. The growing popularity of golf has scarcely abated since. Even in times of economic downturn, the game seems to persevere. The marketing director of a sporting-goods company once noted, "Demand for hard goods fluctuates with the economy, but golf balls sell no matter what. One time in Detroit when auto companies were laying off a lot of people, our sales went through the roof. Workers were cashing in their unemployment checks and going to the golf course."

There was a time when the "media" in golf meant a player had a friend from his hometown who hung around the bar with him after the round and called in a few hundred words to the local newspaper later that night. Now, the USGA doles out some 1,600

Bettmann/UPI

badges to news people covering the U.S. Open.

The principal beneficiary of this growing interest has been television—and the tournament sponsors who are attracted to the medium. The ratings for golf on television are not "awesome," as telecasters like to say. The average tournament pulls in about as many viewers as an average baseball game, something under 3 million. But they are generally considered to be good numbers, representing people more likely to buy expensive cars than take the bus. Still, television executives, many of whom play golf themselves, fret over the relatively low numbers generated by their favored pastime. As telecaster and 1965 PGA champion David Marr tried to explain to them, "Golf is a game to be played, not watched."

The official purse money generated by the PGA Tour, a traditional economic indicator of the health of the game in general, has continued to escalate geometrically. Purse money, which stood at $6.7 million in 1970, had doubled by 1980 and then tripled again by 1990. The Ladies Professional Golf Association really got under way with the 1950 season, in which the leading money-winner, Babe Zaharias, took in $14,800, about what a fifteenth-place finish would get a player in the 1992 Centel Classic. In 1960 LPGA players were vying for $200,000 in total purse money; by 1993 they were going for more than $21 million. The financial success of the Senior PGA Tour beggars a press agent's gaudiest dream. In 1979 the Tour did not exist, and PGA seniors spent most of their time sitting on club verandas talking

Russ Halford/Sports Illustrated

Betsy Rawls, Patty Berg, Louise Suggs, and Babe Zaharias (top, left) were big winners in their day; but compared with today's pros, their earnings were a drop in the bucket.

Chi Chi Rodriguez (above), heading home through the San Juan, Puerto Rico, airport in 1964, leaves no doubt as to his prime sponsor's identity.

USGA Collection

about the old days. Less than fifteen years later, they were out on the course fighting for a share of $25 million. Lee Trevino, who toiled in the gold mines of the PGA Tour for more than twenty years to extract some $3.4 million, made more than that in his first five years on the Senior PGA Tour.

The growth of the golf industry, however, should not be measured simply by the rising of traditional indices. Golf professionals make more money than they used to, but so do greenkeepers and caddies.

Golf spawned a wide range of business opportunities that did not exist before the 1950s, then developed a new generation of entrepreneurs to administer them.

Mark McCormack, the creator of IMG, was probably the best golfer ever to come out of the Yale Law School. A scratch player, he qualified for four U.S. Amateur championships, three British Amateurs, and one U.S. Open. Pretty good credentials, but not good enough for a man driven to be the best at whatever he attempts, so McCormack settled for becoming the most powerful agent and power broker in the game. His first agreement was a handshake deal to represent Arnold Palmer, which is still the only contract the two have ever had. McCormack then set about changing the way deals are made between sports figures and corporations. Palmer was given money incentives not only for winning a tournament, but for "trying to win." In 1960 Palmer made $60,000 from McCormack deals. By 1962 he was grossing $500,000, more than six times his on-course earnings.

McCormack struck a vein of corporate lode so rich there

Brian Morgan

In 1958, a handshake agreement between Arnold Palmer and Mark McCormack (top, left, behind Palmer) sealed what would become golf's most lucrative player-agent relationship.

At the 1986 Open at Shinnecock, Arnold Palmer—who had been a spokesman for the USGA Members program since its inception—gets a lift from USGA staffer Karen Bednarski (above).

has been room for every major golfer since then to cash in. In 1990 Lee Trevino simply auctioned himself off to the highest bidder, and when the final bid was opened, he agreed to wear a Spalding visor and play Spalding's irons in return for a five-year contract that paid him $1 million a year. There are dangers in such contracts. Two solid young professionals, Billy Andrade and Andrew Magee, both signed lucrative endorsement contracts with golf-club manufacturers only to find the clubs, however worthy, were ill-suited to their games, and their tournament play suffered as a result. It's the kind of hazard professional golfers don't learn about in college.

McCormack rolls on with more than forty offices in twenty countries. While golf and tennis remain its primary mandates, IMG has moved on to embrace a variety of interests. The sun rarely sets on a day when IMG is not involved in the promotion of something, from the Orange Bowl in Miami to the Asian Snooker Open in Bangkok to a Kiri Te Kanawa recital in Los Angeles.

In 1957 Robert Dedman was a hardworking Dallas lawyer when he decided to go into the country-club business. It was an odd decision, because country clubs had always been run more like garden parties than businesses. The point was to have a good time and not run out of gin; making a profit was considered vulgar. As a result, more than a few American country clubs were going quietly broke. Dedman, however, was developing a few ideas on how to change that. He sensed that the young and increasingly wealthy upper middle class of Dallas would be interested in joining a club, and might lack the patience to wait until death created openings at the more established clubs, such as the Dallas Country Club. The deal he struck with a local land developer was a combination of golf-club and real-estate sales that

Andy Levin

The tram at Waterway Hills in Myrtle Beach, South Carolina (above), transports golfers across the Intracoastal Waterway to the pro shop and first tee.

Driving ranges are big business. More than 6,700 operate throughout the United States; like this complex (below) at the Legends in Myrtle Beach, they're packed, day and night.

would become typical throughout the country for the next thirty years. The developer let Dedman have four hundred acres at fire-sale prices to put up a club and elevate the price of the surrounding lots. The club was Brookhaven, and the operation was so successful that it became the headquarters of Dedman's Club Corporation of America, which now owns and operates two hundred clubs, resorts, and public-fee golf courses around the world.

Combining a club and a real-estate development can bring startling results. Soon after Pete Dye's famous golf torture chamber, PGA West, was put into operation in Palm Springs, California, adjacent housing lots that had been selling for $14,000 began selling for $100,000.

For a long time golf had been something of an afterthought in hotel and resort development. The designation "Championship" pinned to a golf course frequently meant only that the local pro and the hotel's food and beverage manager had once played a $5 Nassau there. Now golf is often a central consideration. The Marriott Corporation first got into the golf business in 1970 when it took over the Camelback Inn in Arizona. The Marriott put in a golf course that it was willing to run at a loss of more than $90,000 a year, if it helped fill rooms. In time, the golf-club operation started turning a profit of $1.6 million a year exclusive of food and beverages. The Marriott people were so taken with such figures that they were soon involved in fifteen more golf properties.

Which is not to say golf is immune from the laws of economics, whatever they are. Although there is a need for more courses to cater to the growing golfing public, a mismanaged golf operation can go just as sour as a misplaced shopping mall. Heeding the call for more golf courses, Florida developers—many of whom understood the game no better than they did the

Andy Levin

Courtesy Pebble Beach Company

uses of the two-iron out of deep rough—built the wrong courses in the wrong places with the wrong financing. They followed all too blindly in the successful wake of the Club Corporation's combination packaging. They figured if they could make money out of one golf course, why not put in two? When the real-estate market turned soft, as it does from time to time, the lots did not sell and the developers were stuck with courses they could not maintain. Inevitably bankers (who understand the game even more imperfectly than developers) wind up in the golf business.

The Landmark Land Co. of Carmel, California, established some of the finest golf-resort properties in America, but when its financial ties to a pair of troubled Louisiana savings and loans were severed by government decree, Landmark skidded badly and was unable to cover its deficits. And so a dozen of our most cherished golf courses, including Kiawah Island, Palm Beach Polo, Oak Tree, Carmel Valley Ranch, Mission Hills, La Quinta, and PGA West, were ticketed to go under the federal auctioneer's hammer.

There can be no more cautionary tale than that of Pebble Beach, which for generations stood as the symbol of all that was best in American golf. The only public facility to host a U.S. Open, Pebble is routinely listed, along with Pine Valley Golf Club in Clementon, New Jersey, as one of the top two layouts in America. Its scenery has inspired poets and artists for centuries, and its attendant acreage is among the most valuable seaside real estate in the land. Until recently, this corporate-and-real-estate combination, which eventually grew to include such nationally known courses as Spyglass Hill and the Links at Spanish Bay, made a fortune for anyone fortunate enough to own it. The area was purchased in 1919 by Samuel F. B. Morse for $1.3 million. In 1978 Twentieth Century Fox, its coffers bulging with the profits from *Star Wars*, bought the operation for $72 million. Three years later the movie company sold out to Colorado oil man Martin Davis. In 1990 Davis off-loaded the property to Minoru Isutani, a Japanese entrepreneur, for $841 million. Even in the euphoria of the times, that was a heart-stopping price. Isutani thought he

Stephen Dunn/Allsport

With golf increasingly popular, new courses were springing up. Here, Samuel F. B. Morse (top, left) takes the controls of a bulldozer during construction of Monterey Peninsula Country Club's Shore Course in 1960.

Payne Stewart (above) follows through, against the Pacific sea spray, at the 1991 AT&T Pebble Beach Pro-Am.

could take Pebble Beach private and sell memberships, mostly to Japanese executives, for $740,000 a crack. If that sounds expensive, remember that at home these same executives were paying up to $2.5 million for a membership that allowed them to play on courses not half as good. You could throw in airfare, hotel bills, and bar chits, and it would still be a bargain. When his idea got stalled in California, Isutani immediately fell behind on his mortgage payments to a Japanese bank and his tax bill to Monterey County. The Sumitomo Bank took control and forced a sale to another Japanese combine for $500 million. In seventeen months Isutani and his investors lost $341 million. One investment banker called it "the most disastrous real-estate deal known to man."

Still, being bunkered is just a temporary reversal, not the end of the world. The game, like the industry it supports, goes on. For the last fifty years, golf has progressed in an apparently ceaseless upward spiral. In 1988 the National Golf Foundation announced that America needed a new golf course every day of the year until the dawn of the twenty-first century to accommodate all the new golfers coming into the game. At the time, it seemed a lunatic idea based on unreasoned hope rather than economic possibility. Surprisingly, though, something fairly close to that happened. In the next five years, some 1,500 courses went into operation.

Overseas, the figures are even more dramatic. In Sweden—where it is too cold to wash your car much of the year, let alone play golf—the number of active golfers more than quadrupled in fifteen years. Who knows where the frenzy will strike next? In the early 1990s there was an enormous boom in golf-course construction in Thailand, which suddenly sprouted almost twenty new courses. Then the construction crews moved on to a suddenly golf-mad Malaysia.

Golf was first a game for rough-hewn Scots trying to figure a way to get someone else to pay for their drinks. Then it became an outdoor pastime for the gentry. Now it has become inexorably woven into the fabric of popular sport. Like the yips, once it gets you, it never lets go.

Aaron Chang

Each day, some 65,000 balls are struck at the thirty-two practice tees at Ala Wai Golf Course in Honolulu.

The Celebrity Player

I would rather open on Broadway in Hamlet with no rehearsals than tee off at Pebble Beach.

—Jack Lemmon

In 1931 Bobby Jones set out to teach golf to Hollywood. He shot eighteen films for Warner Brothers, instructing the likes of W. C. Fields, James Cagney, Edward G. Robinson, and Loretta Young. The series was shown in movie houses across America to more than 20 million people. Those classic shorts disappeared in the 1940s. Eventually, a single copy was found in a Georgia bank vault.

What has never vanished is the fascination celebrities have for the game. Like the rest of us, these men and women lack the skill and strength to pitch to Babe Ruth, play tennis with Chris Evert, or go one-on-one with Michael Jordan. But on some of America's most challenging courses, notably Pebble Beach, Jackie Gleason has taken a skin from Arnold Palmer, and Michael Jordan has been seized by the dream of another career as a professional golfer.

The pro-am came into full flower when Bing Crosby began staging his fabled Clambake at a California resort in 1937. And when television began tagging along to record the high jinks, Gleason, Bob Hope, Dinah Shore, and a dozen others decided to host events of their own.

Indeed, some celebrity golfers have been

Culver Pictures

Stephen Rose/Gamma Liaison

2

John Russell/Gamma Liaison

3

The Bettmann Archive

4

good enough to compete in national championships. Ruby Keeler qualified for the Senior Women's Amateur. Crosby drew 20,000 spectators when he played against a carpenter in the 1950 British Amateur at St. Andrews (apparently mortified at the commotion he was causing, Crosby decided to blow his lead and disappear in defeat).

A politician's golfing ineptitude can become a cruel metaphor for the man, as President Ford quickly found when he beaned a spectator. But in a kinder, gentler era, President Eisenhower (an eighteen-handicapper with a chronic slice) played the game with such endearing passion he taught a generation of Americans the pleasures of the sport.

1 And away we go—Arnold Palmer and Jackie Gleason at Shawnee Country Club in Pennsylvania in the early 1960s.
2 Bill Murray at the third annual Robert F. Kennedy Memorial Golf Tournament at Hyannisport Club in Massachusetts.
3 Tennis star Andre Agassi in Las Vegas.
4 Leo Diegel, Joe Turnesa, and Maureen Orcutt (left to right) observe Babe Ruth's style at a benefit for Al Smith's failed Presidential bid in 1928.

Phil Stern

5

Archive Photos/London Daily Express

6

Archive Photos

7

5 *Bob Hope with Bing and Kathryn Crosby and one of their budding young golfers in London while filming* **The Road to Hong Kong** *in 1961.*

6 *Rita Hayworth practices putting in Spain in 1963.*

7 *Clark Gable at MGM director Frank Borzage's Golf Tournament at the California Country Club in 1947.*

8 Beverly Hanson, Helen Dettweiler, Katharine Hepburn, Betty Hicks, and Babe Zaharias (left to right) during filming of Pat & Mike in 1952.

9 Fred Astaire with Mrs. Hortense Lowits at a miniature golf course atop a Manhattan hotel.

10 Michael Jordan, at the 1987 Fred Meyer Golf Challenge in Portland, Oregon, is a big pro-am draw.

11 Peter Falk, at Riviera Country Club in Pacific Palisades, California.

Culver Pictures

8

The Bettmann Archive

9

Brian Drake/SportsChrome

10

Eric Sander/Gamma Liaison

11

12 George Bush on the course at Kennebunkport, Maine, shortly after the start of the Gulf War.

13 William Howard Taft chose golf as his game; it was "in the interest of good health and good manners."

14 Woodrow Wilson, who played in street shoes, carried a cloth "Sunday bag" and only a few clubs.

15 A big tipper of caddies, Warren G. Harding, the best of the early President-golfers, often played with Grantland Rice and Ring Lardner.

16 Dwight D. Eisenhower at Gettysburg in 1961. Ike put a green on the White House lawn and vacationed at Augusta.

Brad Markel/Gamma Liaison

12

USGA Collection

13

USGA Collection

14

The Bettmann Archive

15

Burt Glinn/Magnum Photos

16

Bettmann/UPI

17

Andy Hayt/Sports Illustrated

18

Photofest

19

17 John F. Kennedy, at the first tee at the Hyannisport Club in 1963 with his sister, Pat Lawford.

18 Gerald R. Ford, his handicap in the mid-teens, likes to compete in pro-ams. After a few spectators were struck by errant Ford drives, Bob Hope said, "Ford made golf a contact sport."

19 Richard M. Nixon (handicap: fourteen) in the late 1950s.

20 President Bill Clinton at Farm Neck Golf Club in Martha's Vineyard, Massachusetts, in 1993.

Bettmann/Reuters

20

The Pat Hathaway Collection

21

Courtesy Pebble Beach Company

22

The Bettmann Archive

23

21 Bing Crosby (handicap: two) on the seventeenth at Pebble Beach.

22 Elizabeth Taylor and Conrad Hilton, Jr., honeymooning at the Lodge at Pebble Beach in 1950.

23 Jean Harlow.

24 Rosalind Russell, circa 1939.

25 Jack Lemmon in his Hollywood home in 1955. An avid golfer, Lemmon often appears in the Pebble Beach Pro-Am; he's never made the cut.

26 Clint Eastwood at home in California in 1958.

27 Ruby Keeler, circa 1938, in Palm Springs, California.

28 Arthur Ashe at the Pebble Beach Pro-Am.

Photofest

24

John R. Hamilton

25

John R. Hamilton

26

Photofest

27

Courtesy AT&T Pebble Beach Pro-Am

28

29

Courtesy Jack Scagnetti

Archive Photos

30

Long Photography Inc.

31

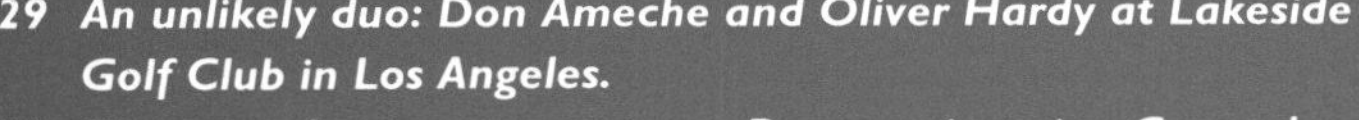

29 *An unlikely duo: Don Ameche and Oliver Hardy at Lakeside Golf Club in Los Angeles.*

30 *Photographers concentrate on Dagmar, ignoring General Hoyt Vandenberg and Tony Martin in 1951.*

31 *Dean Martin at Pebble Beach in 1971.*

32 *Ninety-one-year-old John D. Rockefeller at his private golf course at Ormond Beach in Florida, in 1930.*

33 *Tip O'Neill at the 1990 Bob Hope Desert Classic in Palm Springs.*

34 *Bob Hope rolled out his $12,000 golf cart, including a videotaping system to record his game, at his 1971 Desert Classic.*

Bettmann/UPI

32

Robert Tringali/SportsChrome

33

John R. Hamilton

34

The Bettmann Archive

The Clubhouse

Curt Sampson

Previous spread: The clubhouse at Newport Golf Club, host club to the first official Amateur and Open championships in 1895. In 1995 the club will be the site of the Amateur championship, but the clubhouse won't appear the same; the wing to the right was destroyed in a 1953 hurricane.

On the patio of The Country Club in Brookline, Massachusetts, founded in 1882, Jess Sweetser (above) is presented the trophy for his 1922 Amateur win.

IF GAMES ARE A UNIVERSE, CLUBS ARE ITS PLANETS. PEOPLE WHO like to hunt quail, sew quilts, or play quoits are drawn to each other and form their own little worlds. If golf is your passion, however, you require more than just the company of other golfers and the game itself. You also need a place to hang your coat, store your shoes, put on your golf boots, make your bets, settle your bets, have a drink. You need a clubhouse.

Even more than the golf course, the clubhouse defines the character of the membership. Are we frugal or extravagant? Traditional or avant garde? Social or narrowly focused on golf? An early classic of the make-do style was the first permanent clubhouse, at Westward Ho! in Devon, England, circa 1864. It was called The Iron Hut. A tiny round structure covered with a rusty metal roof, it was barely big enough for a table, a few chairs and a bar. After their rounds, weary Westward Ho! golfers stored their sticks in the rafters. You can almost smell the wet wool, almost taste the whiskey.

A very different kind of clubhouse has reached full expression 130 years later. At the Las Colinas Sports Club in Irving, Texas, the hut has become a palace, the wool has been replaced by Spandex. "One of the nation's most complete and multifaceted sports clubs," the promotional brochure says, and undoubtedly it is, though the thirty-six holes of golf attached to it seem no more important than the twelve Plexipave tennis courts, the cushioned indoor jogging track, the four restaurants, the two bars, the indoor lap pool, the day-care center, the Gravitron machines in the workout room, or the fifteen staff trainers, six of whom, you are told, have master's degrees in exercise physiology, to help you tone your "nine major muscle groups." Isn't that Herschel Walker, the pro football player, standing in front of a full-length mirror watching himself lift absurdly heavy dumbbells? It is.

Is this what we've come to? the purist may ask. What did the game's pioneers know or care about the nine major muscle groups, much less Plexipave and Gravitron? But this attitude assumes an earlier Age of Innocence, when pioneer clubhouses were built of sod or sticks. In fact, however, some of the earliest

Reporters gather around Ben Hogan in the Oakmont locker room after his fourth and last Open victory in 1953. Also, for a fourth and last time, Sam Snead finished second.

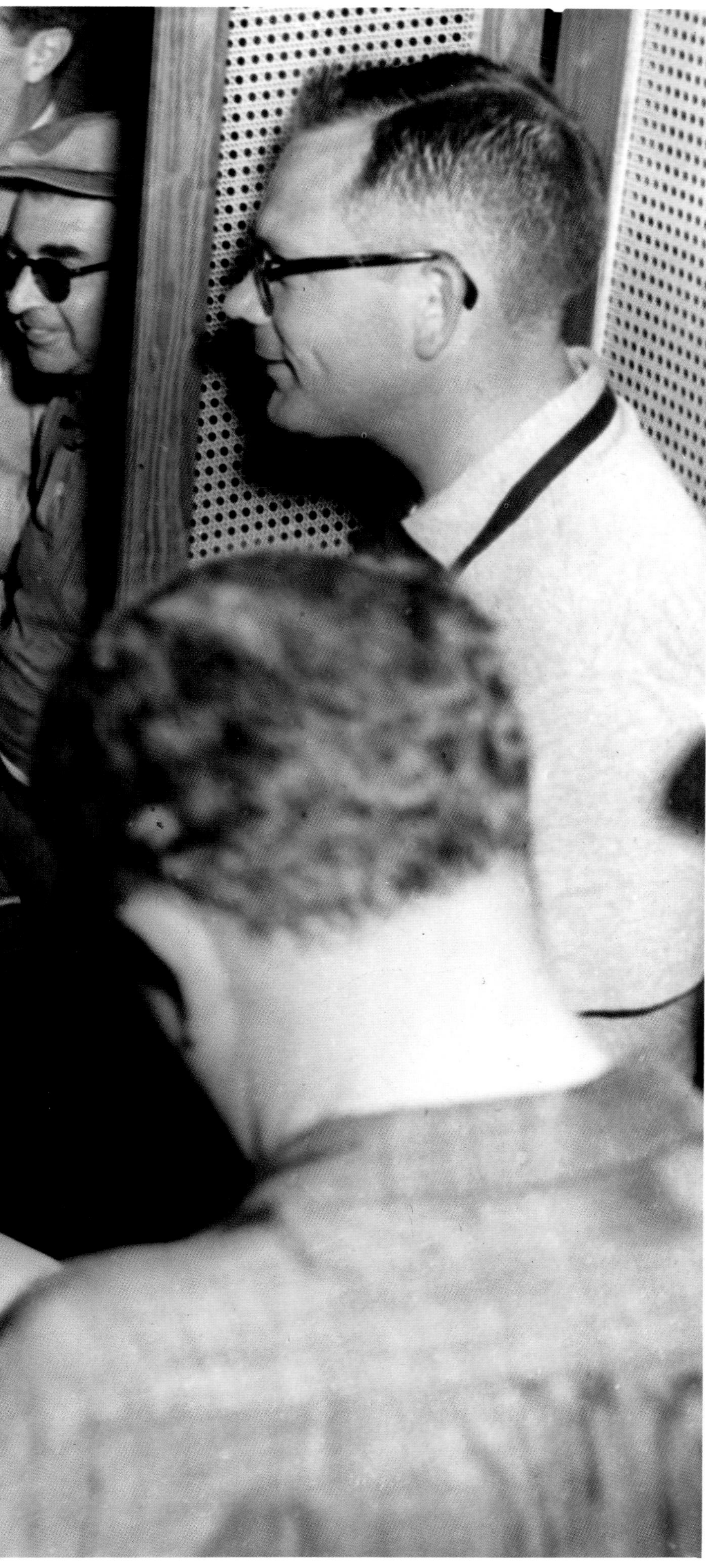

Globe Photos

American golf clubhouses were posh places suitable for debutante balls and weddings, and served concurrently as headquarters for aficionados of polo, curling, croquet, and cricket. Moreover, those who mourn The Iron Hut and what it represented are missing the bigger picture: The nuts and bolts of clubhouse organization and architecture are far less interesting, far less important, than the people inside the buildings.

DAY AFTER DAY, HE SITS BY THE WINDOW, ERECT AND UNMOVING, a Buddha in a business suit. No one sits near him, ever. Occasionally, a shaft of sunlight glints off his glasses and illuminates his white shirt and the swirl of blue smoke around his head. Then the beam recedes and Ben Hogan returns to the shadows.

His club is Shady Oaks in Fort Worth, Texas. His clubhouse is a wide, spread-out affair, all Frank Lloyd Wright horizontal lines and glass. Hogan's best friend, Marvin Leonard, built it in 1958, when their previous course, Colonial, which Leonard built across town in 1936, was no longer as private as either man would like. Their portraits hang in the lobby, on either side of a huge, brown-and-green-tile mosaic of a live oak tree. The tycoon, posed with a golf club, looks somewhat stiff; the golf champion appears relaxed and friendly, a cigarette held casually between two fingers of his right hand.

Some old men live out their days fishing with an unbaited hook, staring quietly at the play of light on water, contemplating their mortality or what to have for lunch. Hogan prefers to stay close to the game that consumed him. His corner of the nineteenth hole juts out like the prow of a ship, insinuating itself slightly onto the golf course. From there the silent man can see everything on the ninth and eighteenth fairways and greens.

"Hogan's watching you" is the best three-word psych-out in sports. Once someone whispered the magic words to a visiting professional basketball coach, a big guy, an ex-player, a battle-hardened referee baiter. The coach promptly skulled his chip to the ninth green forty yards past his target. Now his ball was practically in Hogan's ashtray, and the Hawk couldn't fail to notice him. With a stricken look, the coach chopped again—and hit so far behind the ball that his divot flopped over it, covering it in a blanket of earth and grass.

SEMINOLE GOLF CLUB IN NORTH PALM BEACH, FLORIDA, WAS opened on New Year's Day, 1930, revealing a "Men's Hall" configured exactly like the nave of a church. "Magnificently constructed," said *Palm Beach Life* magazine, "with the enormous cypress beams of the gable ceiling, the modulated plaster of the walls and the panels of fine-grain pine which form the lockers . . . Sunlight filtering through the lofty windows placed in niched recesses lends a mellow sheen to the lockers and the deep hued wood of the floor."

Golf is not a religion, of course, and clubhouses are not

Robert Walker

temples. Still, in the hush of Seminole's men's locker room you feel a serenity that might be divine. Through half-closed eyes, the founding fathers appear. There's Donald Ross, the immortal designer of the golf course, standing at the bar with a foursome of founding members—Hutton, Chrysler, Vanderbilt, and Pulitzer—discussing his creation and their golf games. By a locker is Hogan, young and handsome; he spends the month of March here, preparing for The Masters. That's Dave Marr, the boyish assistant pro, explaining why the place is so quiet this morning: "No one shows up at Seminole until the crack of noon." Other presences can be imagined as players in the Seminole Amateur–Professional, a big-time event from 1937 to 1961. The 12:18 starting time in 1948: on the first tee, Porky Oliver and the Honorable Joseph P. Kennedy, handicap thirteen; off ten, Bobby Locke and His Royal Highness the Duke of Windsor, an eighteen.

DENNIS REDMOND BUILT THE BIG, WHITE HOUSE ON A HILL overlooking his Augusta, Georgia, indigo plantation in 1854. A graceful, three-story, porch-encircled mansion, it had two unique architectural features: It was the first home in the South built with concrete walls, and it had an eleven-foot-by-eleven-foot cupola in its center, with windows on all sides. Slaves working in the fields below might look up and see the master surveying the scene from his glass-walled aerie.

The elitist feel of the place did not disappear when it became a golf course in 1933; that sense was, in fact, perpetuated, even enhanced, by the founders of the new enterprise, Bobby Jones and Clifford Roberts. Given the patrician attitudes of Jones and Roberts, together with the enormous popularity of and continued reverence for Jones and The Masters, Augusta National couldn't have turned out any other way. Augusta is a national golf shrine, with a course most of us cannot play and a clubhouse we cannot use.

Unless, of course, you are a member, or it is Masters week and you are a contestant or a past champion. Amateur invitees to the tournament may even bunk in the cupola room—everyone calls it the Crow's Nest—which was remodeled in 1945 into a small dormitory: six single beds, one bathroom, kelly green carpet, white painted walls. Another Masters tradition, the Champions Dinner, was started in 1952 by Hogan, out of relief and gratitude at finally winning the event the year before after several near misses. Only Masters champions and one or two club officials may attend.

"That dinner's not as much fun as you might imagine," says one former champion. "That Hord Hardin [a former Augusta National president]—what a wet blanket! Cliff Roberts was

The elegant and comfortable locker room at Seminole Golf Club, in Florida (left), has echoed to the banter of Chryslers, Pulitzers, Vanderbilts, the Duke of Windsor—and Ben Hogan, who keeps a locker here.

4 3 5 4 5 3 4 4
Green
Scores
On A

Bettmann/UPI

Tony Roberts

Arnold Palmer (left) towels down in the Augusta National locker room during the 1961 Masters. For the first time, play was canceled for an entire day because of the drenching rain.

The Augusta National clubhouse (above), built in 1854, originally was the "great house" at Fruitlands Plantation.

worse. And Jones would give you a look if you spoke out of turn."

A visitor to Augusta National Golf Club notices that the clubhouse is wide but not deep, surprisingly light and airy inside, with décor and furnishings far more functional than opulent. It is not an art gallery, nor is it a trove of memorabilia. The locker room is unexceptional, and there is no real bar. None of that matters much; people, and memories of people, are the key here. The antebellum courtesy of the waiters washes over you. They find out your name: "What would you like to drink, Mr. Smith? Yessir, yessir." Outside, there is one of the greatest courses in the world, and on a wall, in a glass case, are Bobby Jones's clubs. That is enough.

THE MUTED FOOTFALL OF GUCCI LOAFERS ON THICK CARPET, the murmur of polite conversation in a large dining room—these are the sounds of the private clubhouse. The noises of the daily fee course where I grew up were quite different. I can still hear the sharp scrape of metal spikes on Hush Puppy golf shoes against bare concrete; the sequential pop of scores of beer cans, like small-arms fire at a shooting range; and in the "dining room," a loud, joyous babble of voices. The decibels in the cramped clubhouse reached a crescendo on league nights, meaning any weekday evening during the summer. The leagues were made up of people who bowled together during the winter or worked together every day. There were groups of auto workers, from Ford and Chrysler, as I recall. The Polish Falcons had a league, as did a group from Murray Hill, the Italian neighborhood in nearby Cleveland, and a group of African-American couples from somewhere on the East Side. But the jockeys, trainers, bettors, and bookies from two area racetracks, another subset of loyal customers, were far too disorganized to coalesce.

Auld Da (left, at center), a well-known caddie at St. Andrews Old Course, sold lemon squash and ginger pop from his cart to the likes of Old Tom Morris (on right).

The first clubhouse at Palmetto Golf Club in Aiken, South Carolina (below), circa 1900. It was originally built as a farmhouse.

The gabled clubhouse at Essex County Club in Manchester, Massachusetts (right), home club of the Curtis sisters. Two Women's Amateurs were held there, in 1897 and 1912, the latter won by Margaret Curtis.

Our clubhouse at Boston Hills Country Club in Hudson, Ohio, was an unattractive wooden building with a preposterously low roof, especially in the pro shop. Fortunately, the club seemed to attract short golf professionals. Vally Dirodis and his successor, Bill Shoaf, both stood about five eight, tops. Dark circles ringed Val's eyes, and he had a mournful, basset-hound look, but he was a snappy dresser and was popular with the customers. Bill was a different kettle of fish, stolid, solid, not as good as Val with chitchat. He was a fireman, working twenty-four at the fire station—he was an expert in the maintenance and repair of pump trucks—and forty-eight at the golf course. Bill was color-blind; his wife picked out his clothes, always matching hat, shirt, and pants in identical solid pastels or primary colors—the same cheap clothing he sold in the golf shop. He never quite pulled off the golf look, however, partly because of his shoes, which were the clunky, black, steel-toed safety shoes he wore at the fire station. John "Shorty" Movens, the first-tee starter, was the third pillar of the institution. Shorty was a fedora, a cigar, and eight tobacco-stained teeth. When he reached the punchline of one of his one thousand ethnic jokes, he laughed with a choking sound, and his little plump body convulsed. Shorty fit into the pro shop easily, too. He was four foot ten.

Our men's locker room was funky, gray, and perpetually wet. It reminded me of the train-in-the-rain scene in *Casablanca*. There was a stuffed moose head on a wall; someone—sometimes me—was always stuffing a cigar or cigarette butt in the corner of its mouth.

I returned to Boston Hills a few years ago after a long absence. Vally, Bill, and Shorty, all had died. The old clubhouse had been bulldozed, and a soulless, efficient, metal box had been erected in its place.

THE FIRST CLUBHOUSE OF THE FIRST PERMANENT GOLF CLUB in the United States was a picnic table under an apple tree. The table was manned by a servant employed by Mr. John Reid of Yonkers, New York, who helped found the club in 1888. Reid and the other founders called themselves the St. Andrew's Golf

USGA Collection

Club, but they were soon popularly identified with that tree. They were The Apple Tree Gang.

The informal setup at St. Andrew's recalled the first Scottish clubs, which did not deem four walls to be necessary when other meeting places—that is, bars—were nearby. Leith linksters, for example, refreshed themselves after golf at Luckie Clephan's; Blackheath players met in the Chocolate House and, later, at the Green Man Hotel. At North Berwick, where the local inn was too small to accommodate a big meeting, golfers sometimes gathered in large field tents, where they consumed tons of food and drank oceans of champagne, rum, and Highland whiskey. Thus, the first U.S. club presented nothing new in clubhouses. But seventy-five miles away and across Long Island Sound, Shinnecock Hills started a revolution.

While nearly all golf clubs around the world had borrowed nearby taverns or had adapted local residences as headquarters, Shinnecock Hills built its own. It was the first real clubhouse in the United States, and it was no Iron Hut. Given the wealth and status of those involved, it is no surprise that they didn't just hire a couple of carpenters to erect a mere shelter for their new playground. Instead, they retained an architect, Stanford White. According to historian Alistair Cooke, White was "not by

USGA Collection

any means the most distinguished American architect, but his high-fashion rating was never in question." His most recent project had been Madison Square Garden, and he reportedly regarded this much more modest project on the South Shore of Long Island as a relaxing change of pace. He designed a beautifully proportioned country house, placed on a treeless hill overlooking the twelve-hole course and Peconic and Shinnecock bays. It opened in 1892 and immediately became the social hub of Southampton, a very social town. A year and a half later, Shinnecock became the first golf club to establish a waiting list.

One other feature of the Shinnecock clubhouse was crucial: It served as a private, seven-bedroom hotel. This was an era when country clubs really were in the country, and transportation was by rail and horse and buggy. With golf courses relatively remote and travel so arduous, an overnight stay was often required. Other seminal clubhouses—The Country Club at Brookline, Massachusetts, Chicago Golf Club, and Newport, Rhode Island, Golf Club, for example—also provided rooms for members and their guests.

Professional design, massive size, and hostelry made our first clubhouses costly, which made American golf largely a rich man's game. Herbert Warren Wind described the vicious circle succinctly in his *The Story of American Golf*: "Wealthy men would join a golf course which possessed a well-appointed clubhouse, even if they were not attracted to the game itself . . . . wealthy members were essential if a club was to remain solvent. And unless it could point to a handsome clubhouse, no golf course could hope to attract the women of the community without whose presence the project would not click socially. For these reasons, the golf courses were forced, or thought they were forced, to charge high initiation fees and healthy dues."

Some early clubhouses were masterpieces of understatement, such as the modest facility at Cypress Point. Our golf course is enough, this club seemed to say; our lily needs no gilding. But "big" was the byword of many other notable clubhouses. There were faux châteaux (Newport, Longwood Cricket Club in Boston), brooding Tudor mansions (Baltusrol in New Jersey, Canterbury in Cleveland, Oakmont in western Pennsylvania), gigantic

Tony Roberts

The clubhouse at Shinnecock Hills in Southampton, New York, in 1900 (top left). Built eight years before, it included seven bedrooms for weekend travelers who made the long trip from New York City via horse-drawn carriage or train.

Designed in 1909 by Chester Kirk, Baltusrol's faux-Tudor clubhouse (above) mirrored the aspirations of Louis Keller, the club's founder—and publisher of the Social Register. *The club, along with Oakmont, holds the record for hosting Opens—seven.*

Chi Chi Rodriguez gets his round under way at Medinah Country Club, just outside Chicago. The mock-Moorish clubhouse reflects the ethos of the Ancient Order of the Mystic Shrine, or Shriners, as they are commonly called. In 1922, when construction was completed, only members of the order could join.

wedding cakes (Westchester-Biltmore in Harrison, New York), beached ocean liners (Oakland Hills near Detroit), a self-contained city (Olympia Fields in the Chicago suburbs, which had its own ice-making plant, fire department, and hospital, not to mention seventy-two holes of golf and a dining room that seated eight hundred), fortresses, Gothic cathedrals, and a dream creation from the Shriners—or Aladdin's lamp (Medinah, another Chicago-area club). Some clubhouses featured bowling alleys in their basements. Whether these buildings were examples of wretched excess or monuments to a grander age is debatable.

Perhaps we can all agree, however, that one short-lived convention imported from Britain at the turn of the century was ludicrous: the club uniform. Imagine, if you will, walking into the pro shop at your club and finding your beer-bellied buddies all wearing red broadcloth jackets with bright-green collars and silk embroidery on their lapels (the club dress at Apawamis in New York), or sporting the St. Andrew's ensemble of red coats with bright brass buttons, matching blue-checked caps and waistcoats, and gray knickers with matching spats. Would you laugh or cry?

YOU WOULD CERTAINLY HAVE WEPT IF YOU WERE A MERION member in 1896; or belonged to Olympic in 1906; or to Tacoma Country and Golf Club in 1909; or to East Lake, Bobby Jones's club in Atlanta, in 1914 and again in 1925; or Colonial in Fort Worth, Texas, in 1943 and 1953—all of which burned down. Our early clubhouses were fire traps. It is difficult, in fact, to find an American clubhouse fifty years old or more that has not been reduced to ash and rubble at least once. There is never a good time to have a beloved and valuable structure burn, of course, but the timing of some clubhouse fires was extremely inconvenient. The main building of Chicago Golf Club caught fire ten days before the 1912 U.S. Amateur and was completely destroyed. The upper floor of Inwood Golf Club in Far Rockaway, New York, was destroyed just before the 1923 U.S. Open. Colonial went up in flames a month before the 1953 National Invitation Tournament. All three events, however, were held as planned.

Yet fire was nothing compared with the pair of one-two punches that sent golf and the nation reeling from the teens to the forties: first, World War I and Prohibition; then the Depression and World War II. The Volstead Act meant less revenue from booze, the lifeblood of the private club; the other calamities robbed America of every conceivable resource, including leisure time, money, and human life. Consider this somber reminiscence of Keith LeKander, a former caddie, from a book celebrating Chicago Golf Club's centennial:

"Then came the Depression and the gloom that descended on the golf course, with rumors that some of the members lost their fortunes and some their lives. The caddyshed was overrun with family men trying to earn a few dollars to augment their income."

San Mateo County Historical Museum

Members gaze in dismay at their fire-gutted clubhouse at Burlingame Country Club in California in 1916 (above).

Even the clubhouse roof at Columbia Country Club in Maryland (right) is packed with spectators for a 1942 war charity exhibition match, featuring Open champions: (left to right) Fred McLeod, Craig Wood, scorer Bob Barret, Chick Evans, referee Wiffy Cox, and Bobby Jones.

A flicker of light in the darkness was the golf-course construction organized by the WPA and other government agencies. An outstanding example is the lovely fieldstone clubhouse at the Alix W. Stanley Municipal Golf Links, built by the unemployed men of New Britain, Connecticut, and opened in 1933. After World War II, municipal and daily fee courses, with their more modest club buildings, sprang up like mushrooms after a rain. Golf in the U.S. was no longer a game just for the rich.

THERE ARE NO DEEPER THINKERS ON THE MATTER OF THE clubhouse and its inmates than the people who work there. During their long shifts on the job, attending to the needs of the same clients in the same building day after day, staff members ponder such existential questions as: Who are these people—and why do they act like that? Golf pros are especially apt to classify their members by genus and species. You have, for instance, the Confrontationists—people who can detect the hidden flaw in a beautiful day on a beautiful golf course, and wish to tell you about it; you only hope that they work in quality control for some vital industry. The keen-eyed gentlemen wearing loose-fitting tasseled loafers are the Gin Players. They have cigarette burns on their trousers; they do not have tans. The Fast Players are desperate men—seldom women—who breeze through the pro shop to grab some tees, and judge the day a success if they can play eighteen holes in two and a half hours.

Worst of all are the Round Bores, whose fascination with their own golf overwhelms them. When I was working at a municipal course in Ohio, I was repeatedly regaled by one such sociopath. "On number four," he would drone, "I hit an eight-iron like this, but I missed the putt. Babied it. It was a little uphill, too. Did they mow that green this morning? Next hole . . . ." At

USGA Collection

USGA Collection

this point my eyes would glaze over; on occasion, my breathing would stop. I'd excuse myself, wait on a customer, take and make a few phone calls, re-grip a club, arbitrate a Rules dispute, and read the sports page of the Akron *Beacon Journal.* When I would finally look up, a voice in my ear would be saying, "Then on six, you should have seen the lie I had in the right rough. In some kind of weed, like a dandelion. So I hit a wedge . . . ."

Food and beverage staff know better than anyone that people are more themselves at their club than anywhere else. For example, inhibition seemed not to be a problem for the judge in Houston who, unhappy with the temperature or the quality of the food on his plate, picked up the plate and turned it over; or for the member at a club in Louisiana who drags a ratty, vinyl-covered chair out of the men's locker room to sit on during dinner and drinks, lots of drinks. "Well, I pissed myself again," he announces cheerfully. "Time to go home."

Yet for all their insight into individuals, no caddie, bartender, or golf pro I worked with saw our clubs in context. We never talked about discrimination. A club is a club, we thought, and can include and exclude anyone it wants. I worked at a Jewish club where gentiles were banned, and at a WASP-ish club that didn't allow Jews. Neither club admitted African-Americans, and both gave the back of their hand to women. A reception for new members at Peachtree Golf Club in Atlanta: "And, Barbara, women are allowed to play golf here," an old member told the wife of a new member. "But it is not encouraged." The 1923 PGA Championship at Pelham Country Club: Federico Saraceni would not enter the grounds to watch his son, Eugenio, a professional golfer, because he felt Italians were not welcome. He watched the play on the tenth hole from the street, then walked home. "Yes, it was tough for a little Italian," the boy recalled much later. "The Scots and the English pros didn't like us much." Eugenio Saraceni changed his name to Gene Sarazen.

So is the key to a great clubhouse an atmosphere of equal opportunity and good will to all? Of course not. "It's the locker

Joe Scherschel/Life Magazine

If it wasn't golf, it was cards (top, left): Playing a hand in the locker room are Craig Wood, Lawson Little, Vic Ghezzi, and Tommy Armour, among others.

Ladies' Day at Charlotte Country Club in North Carolina in 1958 (above).

During a rain delay at the 1993 Amateur, David Berganio (above, on left), Public Links champ for that year, deals 'em to Golf World*'s Brett Avery. To the rear are seated John Harris, who would go on to win, and his son Chris; 1991 Amateur champion Mitch Voges catches up on the news.*

Tied at 144 midway through a seventy-two-hole War Bonds match in 1945 at Oakmont, Byron Nelson and Sam Snead (top, right) show they have something else in common—sore feet.

Robert Walker

room," says Byron Nelson. "Especially for a man." His favorites are Inverness in Toledo, The Country Club in Columbus, Ohio, and Champions in Houston. "It's the bar," says Ben Wright, the writer and television golf analyst. "For example, the bar at Winged Foot [in New York] is quite commodious, and absolutely reeks with golf. Country-club activities are far away; you see no sweaty tennis players and dripping swimmers. But my absolutely favorite clubhouse is The Country Club in New Albany, Ohio. It's all you ever wanted—and nothing *more.* These ridiculously opulent places get me down."

It's the view, some say. Henry Longhurst, Wright's British mentor, held that the view from the *bar* is crucial. His favorite was Thunderbird Golf Club in the California desert, which he visited for the 1955 Ryder Cup. "There is a fine view of the mountains a few miles away," Longhurst wrote, "and as the sun sets behind them, a magical peace comes over the scene, as in a tropical twilight, and even our American friends, if they will forgive me saying so, tend to fall silent."

A more scientific opinion comes from Desmond Muirhead, who has designed scores of golf courses and club buildings around the world. He believes clubhouses should be more homelike. "Too many are lofty, drafty, and pretentious," he says. "Any sense of camaraderie is lost . . . . a clubhouse should be a home, not a mausoleum."

What Muirhead has in mind can be found in a lovely, tree-shrouded frame house in Roanoke, Texas. Deep couches and chairs surround the main room, and a large window reveals an appealing view of the greenery outside. There is some original art—a bronze in this corner, an oil painting in that. There are golf memorabilia, too, including a replica of a plaque at Augusta National. "Byron Nelson Bridge," it reads. "Dedicated April 2, 1958, to commemorate Byron Nelson's spectacular play on these two holes (12-13) when he scored 2-3 to pick up six strokes on Ralph Guldahl and win the 1937 Masters Tournament." This is a cozy place, a pleasant refuge. There is only one problem with it:

It is not a clubhouse. It is Byron and Peggy Nelson's living room.

My ideal clubhouse would combine San Francisco Golf Club with The Ocean Course at Kiawah Island, South Carolina. Among the endearing qualities at SFGC are its wonderfully dowdy locker room (imagine it is 1930 again and you're at the local Y); the membership's abject love for the traditional game of golf (former USGA presidents Grant Spaeth and Sandy Tatum belong to the club, and twenty-two members belong to the R&A); and its masterpiece of a golf course. The Ocean Course, site of the 1991 Ryder Cup, is the toughest track in the world. After a round there from the back tees on a windy day, I imagined my brain resembled the barrel of live eels I once saw outside a restaurant in Korea. But the clubhouse restored my sanity. No holes are visible from the picture windows, just an unobstructed look at the practice putting green, and beyond it a flat green plain, sand dunes, and the soothing, hypnotic, breaking waves on the beach. After the contemplation of this scene and several malt beverages, I was myself again.

A smiling Frank Walsh is the front-runner after the second round of the 1940 Open at Canterbury, but Lawson Little would take the trophy, while Walsh tied for tenth.

ttmann Archive

The Amateur Champion

Jaime Diaz

Previous spread: Glenna Collett Vare still holds the record with six Women's Amateur championships. Here, at an exhibition in the late 1920s, she approaches the sixth green at Pebble Beach.

Bill Campbell (above), later to become USGA president and captain of the R&A, accepts the champion's trophy at the 1964 Amateur at Canterbury Golf Club in Cleveland.

USGA Collection

WILLIAM CAMPBELL HAS WORKED FIVE DAYS A WEEK FOR forty-seven years in his comfortably cluttered Huntington, West Virginia, insurance office, the office that was his grandfather's before him. But Campbell has played competitive golf even longer, appearing for the forty-seventh time in 1993 in his state amateur.

Perhaps better than any living golfer, this tall, lean man, now in his eighth decade, personifies the amateur champion. He is the only person to have served both as president of the United States Golf Association and as captain of the Royal & Ancient Golf Club of St. Andrews. And he can recount his heartbreaking loss in extra holes in the 1954 British Amateur final and his 1964 U.S. Amateur victory with equal fondness.

Campbell decided long ago that "it's not the winning that is so much fun . . . it's the trying. We react to the white hot heat of pressure in different ways, but one is to enjoy the aliveness of it all." That's one reason that Campbell still looks forward to the West Virginia Amateur every summer. "It is like a bell ringing and I water at the mouth," he explains. "I love it because that's where I got to know golf. Someone said, 'Bill, how can you, now that your abilities have faded, how can you enjoy it?' But I'm of the school that relishes these things. You get turned on by situations that demand of you more than you have. In the effort, you often become your best self."

The golfers appearing in the U.S. Amateur nowadays are mostly college students. Unlike Campbell and the top U.S. amateurs until the 1960s, they are professionals in training, practicing or playing seven days a week. Thirty years ago the USGA revised the Rules of amateur status to accommodate this new generation.

A case can be made—and it is a rather persuasive one—that these young men and women who will make careers in golf rather than insurance or some other profession do not spend enough time competing as amateurs to discover their best selves. Still, golf serves as an effective baptism. Young people are com-

USGA Collection

pelled to live by the gentleman's code of a Bobby Jones or a Bill Campbell: They learn how to win, how to lose, how to deal with their emotions, how to summon courage, how to understand the folly of cheating, how not to quit. Golf is not rewarding if it is not a test of character as well as skill. Its champions want to keep it that way.

Deane Beman, the longtime commissioner of the PGA Tour, who had a vested interest in seeing young amateurs make professional golf their career, argues for the lessons learned in top-flight amateur tournaments. Beman, who won the Amateur in 1960 and 1963 and played head-to-head with Jack Nicklaus throughout his teens and early twenties, says, "I think about those days all the time. You realize what an enjoyable adventure you had and how much what you made yourself is part of your life."

As for Nicklaus, he says, "I think the spirit of amateur golf—to play for the game itself and to play it with integrity—that's never left me. I would have been out of the game much sooner if it had. I still love to compete, to test myself, to play the game. That is the real lesson of champions like Bob Jones, and it's stayed deep inside."

Trophies to the winners: Players sign up for the* The Washington Post *Junior championship at Manor Country Club in Maryland.

Seventeen-year-old Jack Nicklaus (right), by dint of a hometown win, adds another trophy to his shelf.

USGA Collection

USGA Collection

At the Apawamis Club in Rye, New York, Amateur champion Walter Travis (above) stands over a putt in his semifinal match with Charles Seeley at the 1901 Met Amateur. Seeley would best "The Old Man" but lose to Findlay Douglas in the final.

Caddies Irving Hackett, Ed Hart, Joe Carew, and Phil Fahey (right) carry both bag and flag for their charges at an exhibition at Winchester Country Club in Massachusetts.

UNDER THE RULES DRAWN UP BY THE USGA IN THE 1890s, the definition of an amateur was carefully calculated. To qualify as a competitor in the U.S. Amateur championships at the turn of the century, a person could not have caddied past the age of fifteen or within five years of entering the competition. Nor could he have wagered in a match with a professional, given a lesson for money, or been paid for assisting in the building of a golf course.

"The founders may have been citing the ancient Greeks in posing this amateur ideal," observes former USGA president Grant Spaeth, "but in fact they were constructing a very elaborate way of keeping the lower classes out of their clubs."

A reporter for the *Providence Journal* who covered the first American Amateur championship in 1895 openly mocked the event as "a rather senseless and rich man's game." And there was truth to the charge that it was the avocation of the wealthy. The early amateur champions, men of leisure like Walter Travis and Jerry Travers, prized the game's code of ethics and behavior. That was their legacy. But it was Bobby Jones who gave golf the mystique that only a genius could impart. Handsome, gracious, gifted with supernal skill and a fighting spirit, Jones came to embody the idea of a champion.

From 1923 to 1930, neither Gene Sarazen nor Walter Hagen, the two leading professionals of the day, won a championship in which Jones was entered, while Jones won the U.S. Open four times and the British Open three times. In those eight years, during which he remained a part-time golfer, Jones added five U.S. Amateur championships and one British Amateur for a total of thirteen major championship titles. Only Nicklaus, with twenty titles spread over twenty-seven years, has won more.

It was a career that ended with an incredible flourish:

The Bettmann Archive

Marines escort Bobby Jones to the first tee at Merion for the 1930 Amateur (above). It would be the final victory in his Grand Slam.

More uniformed escorts, but British this time (top, right): Jones walks off the course after besting Roger Wethered in the final of the 1930 British Amateur.

USGA Collection

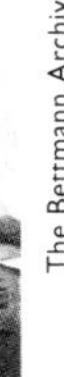

Jones won eight of the last eleven championships in which he played, and was runner-up in one of the other three. The culmination, of course, was the Grand Slam in 1930, when he won, in order, the British Amateur, the British Open, the U.S. Open, and the U.S. Amateur.

A Chicago sportswriter, drawing on Grantland Rice's famous description of the Notre Dame backfield, wrote of the final contest: "There goes another race by the Four Horsemen of the Apocalypse over the fairways of Merion, and this time their names are Jones, Jones, Jones, and Jones." Jones retired at the age of twenty-eight.

"What he did was create a model that everyone, consciously or unconsciously, followed," Bill Campbell points out. "It is why we have had so many fine people in golf. Has there ever been a better loser than Jack Nicklaus? He liked losing the least of anyone, but he handled it better. That kind of behavior goes back to Jones. He showed the world how to do it."

Jones arrived at that exemplary point only after a considerable struggle with internal demons. Early in his career, he could fall prey to fits of rage on the golf course, which left him ashamed and others in doubt as to whether he would ever be able to achieve the self-control that a champion must have. Golf writer Al Laney, who became a lifelong friend of Jones's, admitted that on several occasions, he had been "frightened" by the young golfer's temper. "He knew well that he was poisoning himself with anger, that he must find the inner strength to rise above it," Laney wrote. "To reconcile this side of his nature with the wonderful young person I knew was a difficult thing for me."

In 1921, after Jones seethed with anger at his performance at the Old Course at St. Andrews on the eleventh hole of the third round in the British Open, he vowed to change. Within months, he had subdued his demons and become a model of decorum. By the mid-1920s, when Jones was the favorite at every event he entered, even the pros he was beating respected and were genuinely fond of the college-educated, country-club boy. "Bob was a fine man to be partnered with in a tournament," wrote Gene

Archive Photos

FPG

At The Greenbrier in West Virginia, Glenna Collett (left) would capture the first of her Women's Amateur championships, defeating Englishwoman Mrs. Gavin soundly in the 1922 final, 5 and 4.

An unidentified woman films the putting stroke of four-time Curtis Cup member Maureen Orcutt (above).

Sarazen in his autobiography. "He made you feel you were playing with a friend, and you were."

The antithesis of the self-absorbed athlete, Jones was totally candid about his own frailties. He revealed that the strain of competition caused him to lose as much as eighteen pounds during a playing week, and he regarded his tendency to lose concentration once he was in the lead as a significant weakness. He never pretended to have conquered the game. On the contrary, he was both humbled and fascinated by its mystery.

"You learn very soon, I think, in tournament golf, that your most formidable adversary is yourself," he wrote in *Golf Is My Game*. "You win or lose according to your own ability to withstand pressure. You must learn to keep on playing your game despite all the disturbing thoughts that may keep crowding in upon your consciousness, and, above all, you must keep fighting the awful pressure, no matter how much you would like to give in to it."

"I think of Jones in terms of two halves of a perfect person," says Grant Spaeth. "This uncanny balance of furious competition performed in the most gracious manner. And a life utterly devoid of arrogance. I think that is really the standard of the amateur champion."

WHILE BOBBY JONES WAS ADVANCING THE MEN'S GAME, TWO extraordinary players were elevating the standard of the women's game.

In America, Glenna Collett changed the women's game from one played carefully but unspectacularly along the ground to a soaring version contested through the air. An artist with her fairway woods, Collett won the U.S. Women's Amateur a record six times, the first in 1922 at the age of nineteen, the last as Glenna Collett Vare in 1935 against seventeen-year-old Patty Berg. She competed in the championship as late as 1958. Today the LPGA annually gives the woman with the lowest scoring average the Vare Trophy.

Across the Atlantic, Joyce Wethered, who never competed in America, won the English Ladies' Championship the only five times she ever played in it, and the Women's British Amateur four times. In those events, the only two championships in which she played, Wethered won an astounding total of thirty-six of thirty-eight matches.

Jones, who played an exhibition with Wethered at St. Andrews in 1929, said he had never felt so outclassed. "It was not so much the score she made as the way she made it," he wrote. "Other male experts would likely have made a better score, but one would have expected them to miss shots. It was impossible to expect that Miss Wethered would ever miss a shot—and she never did."

For decades women's careers in golf were hampered by the belief that no properly brought-up young woman would even consider a life of competition away from home. In 1937 prominent amateur Maureen Orcutt, then thirty years old, wrote an article in *The American Golfer* in which she warned women away from competitive amateur golf. It was titled "It's Not Worth It!"

"Traveling all over the country from California to Florida is an expensive and, generally speaking, futile way of spending one's time and money," Orcutt wrote. "How much better for that girl if her father were to invest the thousands of dollars he intends to put into her golf game so that she may enjoy a more stable career in some productive line. She'll probably be a lot more happy in the end."

Orcutt, of course, was her own best rebuttal: She kept on playing and went on to win the U.S. Women's Senior Amateur in 1962 and 1966.

For women fortunate enough to have the opportunity to play the amateur circuit, the game was its own reward. "We were very earnest," wrote Rhonda Glenn, who competed in amateur golf in the 1950s and 1960s. "We tried very hard. I think now that there was a great deal more to it than glory; it was also that those

On the sand greens of Pinehurst in 1931, Maureen Orcutt (on left) accepts congratulations from three-time Women's Amateur champion Virginia Van Wie, whom she has just beaten in the final of the North and South.

The Bettmann Archive

The Bettmann Archive

In 1931 Francis Ouimet had won the Amateur, but at the next championship it was his turn to congratulate Johnny Goodman (left), who had just taken him in the quarterfinal by 4 and 2 at Baltimore Country Club.

Lawson Little (above) did what no golfer had done before—won both the British and American Amateurs in successive years, 1934 and 1935. Sportswriters called it the Little Slam.

Frank Stranahan (below), honeymoons at Pebble Beach with wife, Ann, in 1954, the year he lost the Amateur to Arnold Palmer. It was Stranahan's last event as an amateur.

The Bettmann Archive

soaring iron shots and pinpoint fairway woods really mattered. Those were different times, and for women the doors of opportunity had opened only a hair. *The Feminine Mystique* was only a gleam in Betty Friedan's eye. This was a chance to achieve, to do this one thing really well."

ALTHOUGH THE AMATEUR GAME REACHED ITS PEAK WITH Jones, the exploits of Lawson Little kept public interest at a high level. With his burly figure, big head, and thick waves of black hair, Little was seemingly built to fill a void, which he did. In 1934 and 1935, the long-hitting Little won both the U.S. Amateur and the British Amateur. In achieving this "Little Slam," and in his undefeated performance in the 1934 Walker Cup, Little won thirty-one consecutive matches in international competition. (Jones's best such streak was fifteen.)

Bold and charismatic as an amateur, Little turned professional in 1936. But he lost his edge as a pro, becoming more interested in the stock market than in the grind of the early tour. He won the 1940 U.S. Open in a playoff with Sarazen, but accumulated the relatively modest total of seven victories as a professional before retiring in 1948. "He never again hit the ball as well or as far as he did in 1934 and 1935," Herbert Warren Wind observed.

The Bettmann Archive

A bon vivant—Charles Price noted that "after winning a tournament, Little was often too busy celebrating to win the next one or perhaps even the one after that, or maybe too busy even to enter it"—Little helped to perpetuate the image of the top amateur as a high-society figure. In his day, amateur championships were conducted on the finest courses, almost always at elite country clubs, while events on the professional circuit were frequently played on ragged public courses for minimal prize money by a barnstorming band of men who worried about how to pay for the next meal and the next tank of gas. And while the pro game received little attention in the press, the results of amateur tournaments like the Western Amateur, the North and South, the Trans-Miss, or even local events like the San Francisco City Championship were big news, and would remain so for years.

The player who represented a new direction for the amateur champion was Frank Stranahan. His was a career unique in the history of golf: Stranahan remained amateur because he could afford to, while at the same time playing regularly on the professional circuit.

The son of a Toledo, Ohio, spark-plug magnate, Stranahan decided—at the age of twelve—to become the best golfer in the world. For the next twenty-five years his life was a great experiment in the manufacturing of a champion. He played and practiced endlessly. Becoming a devotee of the famous body builder Charles Atlas—the Arnold Schwarzenegger of the 1930s and 1940s—Stranahan started lifting weights as a teenager and continued to do so throughout his career. Never satisfied with his technique, he kept moving from one top teacher to another in search of the perfect swing. "Frank had a kind of 'made' swing—it wasn't natural," recalled one of his chief rivals in the amateur ranks, E. Harvie Ward. "But he really worked hard, and he was one of the best I ever saw inside a hundred yards."

Stranahan may have been a rich kid, but he was one with something to prove. His driving intensity was the stuff of a Hollywood movie, one in which the starring role would be played by a young Kirk Douglas.

Bettmann/UPI

Amateur Billy Joe Patton (top, left) led the pack at the 1954 Open at Baltusrol with the only under-par round of the first day. He had lost the Masters earlier that year by one stroke.

Harvie Ward (above) proudly shows Buddy Worsham and Arnold Palmer his scorecard after a course-record-tying 66 in a practice round for the 1949 Amateur at Oak Hill Country Club.

Bettmann/UPI

"Golf gave me the chance to be, instead of being my dad's son, Frank Stranahan the golfer," Stranahan recalled recently. "Then I was the center of attention. And the more attention I got, the harder I worked. I wasn't playing for fun. The ones who are playing for fun can't beat the ones who are working at it."

Besides winning nearly every top amateur event in the United States, Stranahan won the 1948 and 1950 British Amateurs. He also tied for second in the 1947 Masters and in the 1953 British Open. He never won the U.S. Amateur, which was his father's fondest wish, suffering some heartbreaking defeats, including losing the 1950 final to Sam Urzetta on the thirty-ninth hole. Finally, when he lost to twenty-three-year-old Arnold Palmer in the quarterfinals of the 1954 championship, he decided to turn pro.

His mother disapproved of the decision, Stranahan said, "because professionals had no social ranking whatsoever." But for Stranahan, the switch represented another challenge: As long as he had been an amateur, professionals, he felt, had not really respected him. "See, when I would win some event, it was, 'Gee, I'm glad Frank won, but I got the money.' So I decided that if I wanted to be the best player in the world, I would . . . take the money out of their mouths, make them respect me head to head."

However, like Little before him, Stranahan did not have great success as a professional, winning only two official events—the 1955 Eastern Open and the 1958 Los Angeles Open. Shortly after that victory, convinced that he could not become the world's best, he retired from golf to attend Harvard and the Wharton School of Finance.

Stranahan's decision to turn professional represented the beginning of a trend: The best players were starting to look at the pro tour, rather than the amateur ranks, as the place they belonged. After Charlie Coe won the U.S. Amateur in 1949, ten of the next fifteen Amateur champions would go on to turn professional. Although players like Coe and Billy Joe Patton, who nearly won the 1954 Masters, remained amateurs and were a match for almost any pro, younger stars like Gene Littler and Ken Venturi could not resist the enticement of the growing purses, and

Bettmann/UPI

Archive Photos/London Daily Express

Bunker practice for a young Arnold Palmer (top, left), prepping for the 1949 Amateur. He would win the event five years later.

After taking their semifinal matches, Jack Nicklaus (bottom, left) and Dudley Wysong exchange a few words at the 1961 Amateur. Nicklaus won the final easily, 8 and 6, to capture his second title in three years.

Nicklaus (above), with his caddie at his side, lines up a putt at Muirfield, Scotland, during the American rout of the British (9 to 3) in the 1959 Walker Cup.

prestige, of the professional game.

Arnold Palmer's defeat of Robert Sweeny in the 1954 final of the Amateur marked the end of an era dominated by the gentleman amateur. Palmer was the son of a club professional; Sweeny came from a Long Island society family. Isaac B. Grainger, then president of the USGA, vividly remembers giving Palmer the Havemeyer Trophy and seeing the future. "I read some of those great names on the trophy—Francis Ouimet, Bobby Jones, Jess Sweetser, all the rest," Grainger says. "I hoped Arnold would be back the next year to defend his title. We were beginning to lose our Amateur champions because they were quickly turning pro. Arnold said to me after I finished, 'Mr. Grainger, I know what you're referring to, but I'm not going to do it.' But of course, Arnold did do it, very shortly after the Amateur championship."

It was becoming increasingly difficult for top amateurs, particularly those without family money, to stay as sharp as the pros without some sort of arrangement that made it possible for them to play golf all the time. "Some of our patron saints, you can be sure, had patrons of their own who picked up the tab for them in one way or another," wrote former USGA executive director Frank Hannigan in a 1977 "white paper" on amateur golf. "That goes on less today because of the rush to get on the Tour."

One of those who benefited from, but was ultimately undone by this practice was E. Harvie Ward, who won the

At the presentation ceremony of the 1958 Women's Amateur, defending champ JoAnne Gunderson "crowns" Anne Quast, who had just beaten Barbara Romack, 3 and 2, at Wee Burn Country Club in Connecticut.

USGA Collection

Amateur championship in 1955 and 1956. Ward's backer was Eddie Lowery, who owned the San Francisco car dealership where Ward worked. Lowery seemed an ideally sanitized sponsor, having been Francis Ouimet's caddie in the 1913 Open and a member of the USGA's Executive Committee. But when Lowery had tax problems in 1956, he testified on the record that some of his money had gone to pay Ward's expenses.

After a hearing in Golf, Illinois, Ward was suspended by the USGA for one year. He subsequently became a teaching pro and always maintained that he had been unjustly singled out for punishment. "When I saw other guys that were out there playing and they had Wilson golf balls and Wilson bags and Wilson clubs, I mean, you know, come on," Ward said recently. "I think the reason they had to do something was because I was the Amateur champion. If I hadn't been, nobody would have cared."

The Ward episode was a blow to the amateur game, casting doubt on the concept that an amateur could remain pure and still be competitive. In 1956, shortly after a final-round 80 had cost him the Masters by a single stroke, the young Ken Venturi, who had also been sponsored by Lowery, turned professional.

Palmer's success as a professional in the late fifties and early sixties elevated the Tour into a major sports attraction and, with the rise of television, it quickly attracted a national following. The coup de grace to the idea of the career amateur who could compete against the pros came when Jack Nicklaus turned professional in 1962 at the age of twenty-two.

By that time, Nicklaus had won two U.S. Amateurs and had finished second in the 1960 U.S. Open. He had grown up in Ohio revering Jones, who had won the 1926 Open on Nicklaus's home course of Scioto. Nicklaus had always intended to remain amateur, but he soon realized that the world he had envisioned had drastically changed.

"Yes, I was serious about remaining an amateur," he said. "I didn't know how lucrative golf was going to be. I was doing pretty well in the insurance business, making about $24,000 a year at the age of twenty-one. And I was enjoying playing golf. I was being called the best amateur since Bob Jones, and I liked that label. I respected so much what Jones had done."

But by 1961 Nicklaus had a wife and child, and was feeling the squeeze of trying to finish his last year at Ohio State, build his insurance business, and still play amateur golf. "Finally, it was too much to try to put it all together to be as good as I wanted to be. I wanted to be the best I could playing golf, and there was really only one way to do that, and that was to play against the best. That meant being a professional."

He talked to Mark McCormack, Palmer's business manager, who explained to him how he could make $100,000 in his first year by endorsing a variety of products. Nicklaus also consulted Bill Campbell, with whom he had played in the 1959 Walker Cup. Campbell thought Nicklaus would feel less compro-

Larry Petrillo

David Eger (left), the USGA's senior director of Rules and competitions, appeared on two Walker Cup teams and won the 1988 Mid-Amateur.

Jay Sigel (bottom), of Berwyn, Pennsylvania, played in a record nine Walker Cups before turning professional at age fifty to play on the Senior Tour.

Eldrick "Tiger" Woods (right) won an unprecedented three straight Junior Amateur championships.

mised, and be better able to fulfill his destiny, as a professional.

Finally, Nicklaus received a letter from Jones himself. "He said he'd like me to remain amateur and try to do some of the things he had done," Nicklaus recalled, "but that he realized that the allure of turning professional is probably too great today."

In women's golf there was a similar shift. In 1968 JoAnne Gunderson Carner won her fifth Amateur championship by defeating Catherine Lacoste, who the previous year had become the first amateur ever to win the U.S. Women's Open. By the next season Carner had decided that there were no more worlds for her to conquer in amateur golf. In 1969, at the age of thirty, she began playing the LPGA tour.

Since Carner, nearly every top-flight woman amateur has turned professional—among others, Hollis Stacy, who won three Girls' Junior championships; Amy Alcott, who won one; Beth Daniel, who won the 1975 Women's Amateur; Juli Simpson Inkster, who won three straight beginning in 1980; and, more recently, Vicki Goetze, who won the Women's Amateur in 1989 and 1992.

Carner's decision also marked the end of her classic rivalry with fellow Washington native Anne Quast Sander. Carner, the daughter of a carpenter, went to Arizona State on one of the first women's golf scholarships ever given; Sander went to Stanford.

Together, the pair dominated amateur golf. Sander won the Women's Amateur three times—in 1958, 1961, and 1963. She captured the British Women's Amateur in 1980 at the age of forty-three, and took the Senior Women's Amateur in 1987, 1989, 1990, and 1993. In the process, she played more competitive rounds in USGA competitions than any other woman.

The two women were complete opposites—Carner, a robust, relaxed extrovert whose body English could border on the scandalous; Sander, slighter and tightly strung, trying to control her nerves by affecting a cold, emotionless exterior on the course. In the best tradition of amateurism, there was genuine respect and affection between them.

The two first met on a practice green before a junior tournament—Anne thirteen, JoAnne fourteen. "I'll never forget

Lawrence N. Levy/Yours In Sport

Bob Straus

Phil Mickelson (above), three-time NCAA individual champion and winner of the 1990 U.S. Amateur, captured a Tour event—as an amateur.

Stephanie Davis (top, right) endured two extra-hole matches to reach the final of the 1990 Women's Amateur, which she lost to Pat Hurst in yet another overtime match.

Larry Petrillo

Robert Walker

it," Sander told golf writer Rhonda Glenn. "She came right up to me and said, 'Whatcha practicing for? Afraid I'm going to beat you?' "

They played together many times, including three times in the Amateur. The first match was the 1958 semifinal. "I had to make a three-foot, downhill putt to win," Sander recalled. "The ball wasn't in the hole yet, and I swear she threw her arms around me and said, 'I knew you were going to make that one.' "

Such behavior was typical of "The Great Gundy," who combined a rare generosity toward her opponents with supreme athletic arrogance.

"I deep down never wanted to beat anybody real bad," Carner said, in accepting the 1981 Bob Jones Award for sportsmanship. "I had no fear of anything. It did not bother me to three-putt. It did not bother me to hit it in the woods. I always felt that I was better than the person I was playing against. I wish I had that now. For some reason, the minute it said, 'JoAnne Carner, Professional,' I felt I couldn't be as wild as I was as an amateur."

A certain wildness, a lack of inhibitions—what Carner missed—is what the amateur has over the professional. The pro must remain clinically detached to make a living at such a demanding game. The amateur champion can afford to be passionate.

It is the only approach that has ever held any appeal for Bill Campbell. He believes that if he had attempted to turn professional, his passion for the game, combined with his sensitivity, would have worked against him: "I would have been unable to handle it emotionally, that intensity full-time."

Rather, for the amateur champion, competitive golf is something to savor, to preserve in photos, as Bill Campbell does on the walls of his office. Most of all, he explains, it is something to carry inside—"a very private, personal feeling that no one can take away from you.

"That's why I don't worry about the amateur game," Campbell says. "The amateur game belongs to the amateur. It's always been its own reward. And it always will be."

1

The Agony and the Ecstasy

The bleeding is internal in this sport.—Jim Murray

The toll can be fierce. In the course of one Open championship, Bobby Jones lost eighteen pounds. In the 1930 Open, a friend had to cut off Jones's sodden tie with a penknife because he had perspired so heavily that the knot could not be undone.

The misery the game evokes, the physical and mental courage it demands, the rage and exhilaration of the players are the stuff of Greek theater. Even the gods play their parts. Lee Trevino, for one, is certain he will be punished if he has not practiced sufficiently to deserve a win.

The drama of the game, which holds galleries spellbound, is in the testing of its heroes. Take the 1950 Open at Merion: A fiercely determined, front-running Ben Hogan limped into the final nine, his throbbing legs wrapped in heavy elastic bandages. At the twelfth, he leaned heavily on a friend and told him, "I don't think I can finish." Hogan's caddie began to pick his ball from the cup and Cary Middlecoff, with whom he was paired, marked Hogan's ball when necessary. Hogan lost his three-stroke lead in six holes and was forced into a playoff with Lloyd Mangrum and George Fazio. But Hogan's victory the following day was a glorious moment in sport.

Jay Maisel

Phil Sheldon

2

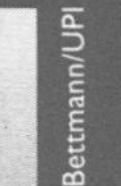

Bettmann/UPI

3

Bettmann/UPI

4

In the 1964 Open, Ken Venturi beat his mental devils and a disintegrating swing to surge into the lead in the third round, but then, dehydrated and ashen-faced, he began to shake and wobble as he moved down the fairways. Venturi has no memory of beginning the final round that afternoon in hundred-degree heat. His pace was a painful crawl and his physical agony was so great that he could not grasp anything more than that he was ahead.

When he sank a long putt for his par on the seventy-second hole, he and twenty-one-year-old Raymond Floyd, with whom he was paired, both began to cry. In joy. In relief.

1 ***Under a blistering sun, Ken Venturi nearly collapsed at the 1964 Open, but rallied for an extraordinary win.***
2 ***Player of the year JoAnne Gunderson Carner at the 1981 LPGA Championship.***
3 ***Lawson Little, triumphant after beating Gene Sarazen in the 1940 Open playoff.***
4 ***Walter Burkemo hugs his Wanamaker trophy at the 1953 PGA Championship.***

Amy Janello

5

Jan Traylen/Phil Sheldon

6

USGA Collection

7

5 Ken Perry takes it hard on the eighteenth at Baltusrol during the 1993 Open.

6 Captain Tom Watson holds aloft the Ryder Cup after the American team's 1993 victory.

7 Margaret Russell is hugged by her dad after winning the Michigan Women's Championship in 1938.

8 Charlie Sifford beams at his first-place finish at the 1969 Los Angeles Open.

9 Nick Faldo is airborne at the 1989 PGA Championship at Kemper Lakes Golf Club.

10 Lee Elder's eighteen-foot birdie falls to give him a sudden-death playoff win in the 1974 Monsanto Open.

11 In the 1970 National Airlines Open in Miami, Lee Trevino groans.

Sheedy & Long/Sports Illustrated

8

Lawrence N. Levy/Yours In Sport

9

Bettmann/UPI

10

Bettmann/UPI

11

AP/Wide World Photos

12

13

John Iacono/Sports Illustrated

14

AP/Wide World Photos

12 Chi Chi Rodriguez dances to a birdie in the "500" Festival Tournament in 1966.

13 Curtis Strange, following in Ben Hogan's footsteps, marches to his second consecutive Open win in 1989.

14 Mary Ann Downey at the 1958 Doherty Women's Amateur in Fort Lauderdale.

15 *Arnold Palmer after blowing a seven-stroke lead in the last nine holes of the 1966 Open.*
16 *Hale Irwin drives to victory in the 1990 Open at Medinah.*
17 *Dave Marr's shining moment at the 1965 PGA Championship.*
18 *Top pro Pat Bradley misses a putt in 1985.*

Walter Iooss, Jr./Sports Illustrated

15

Leonard Kamsler

17

Pete Marovich/Golf Stock

16

Focus on Sports

18

Bettmann/UPI

19

FPG

20

Walter Iooss, Jr./Sports Illustrated

21

USGA Collection

22

John Iacono/Sports Illustrated

23

Bill Fields

24

Focus on Sports

25

19 Louise Suggs urges her putt along at the 1955 Women's Western Open.

20 A family celebration: 1935 PGA champ Johnny Revolta.

21 Ten thousand dollars was top cash for Mickey Wright at the 1966 Ladies' World Series of Golf.

22 Jackie Pung, disqualified at the 1957 Women's Open after signing an incorrect scorecard, feels the pain as Betsy Rawls accepts the top prize.

23 Larry Mize holes a hundred-foot pitch for a sudden-death win over Greg Norman at the 1987 Masters.

24 Payne Stewart seethes over a missed opportunity at the 1993 Open.

25 A misdirected shot winds up in the gallery at the 1984 Open at Winged Foot.

26 Arnold Palmer bides his time at a wet 1991 Bay Hill Classic.

Lawrence N. Levy/Yours In Sport

26

SNEAD +3
LEMA -2
NICHOLS 0

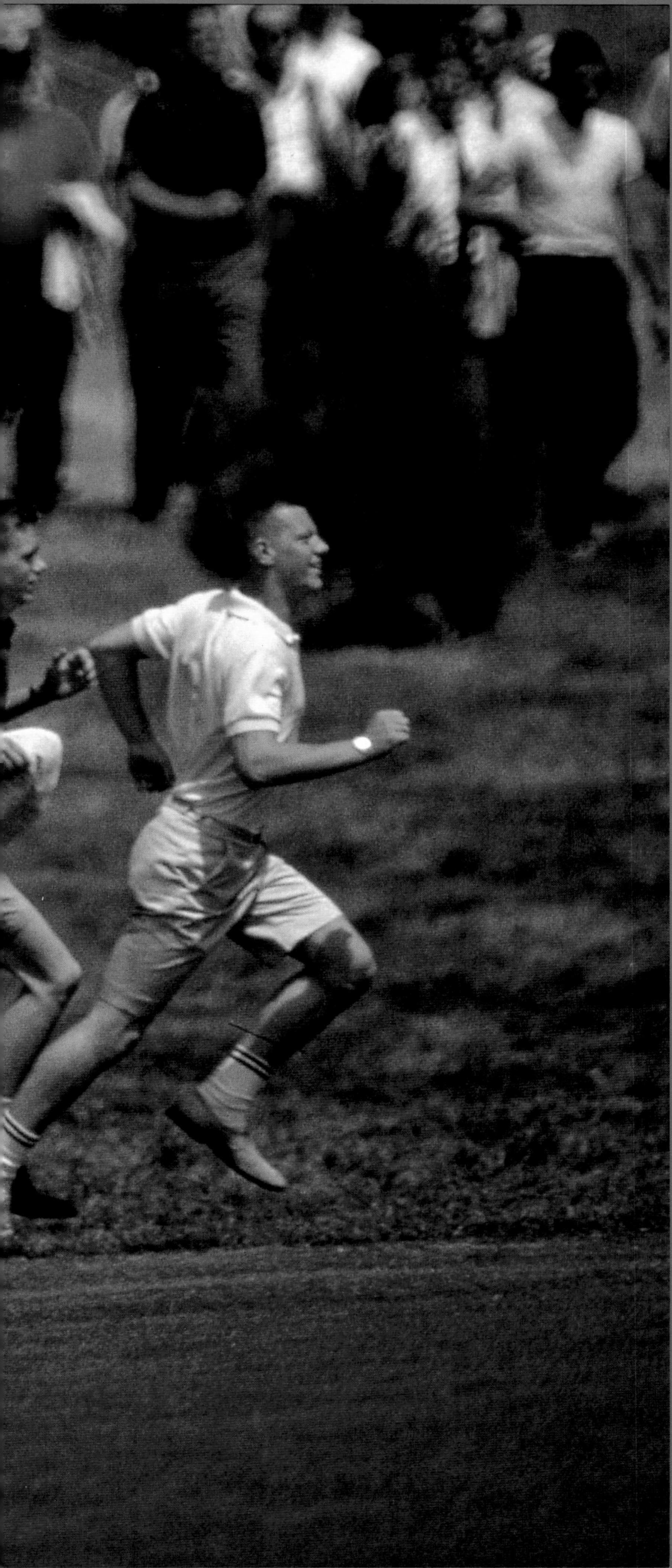

Jay Maisel/Sports Illustrated

John G. Zimmerman/Sports Illustrated

28

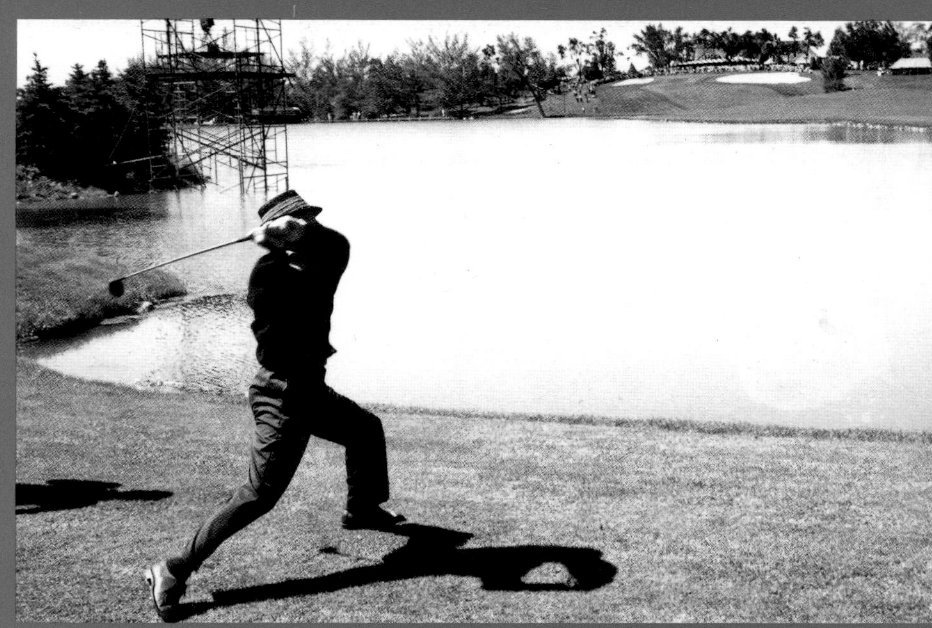

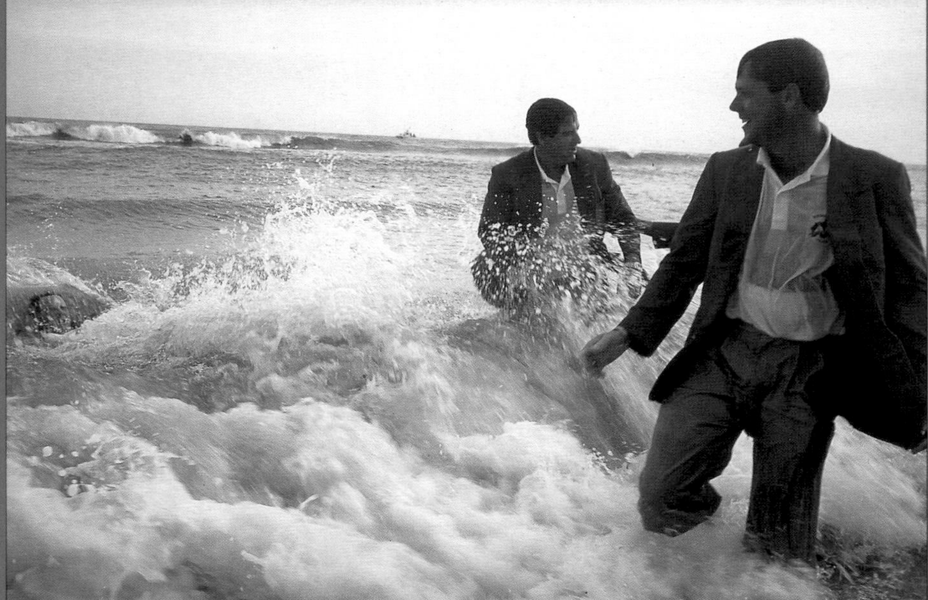

Phil Sheldon

29

Bettmann/UPI

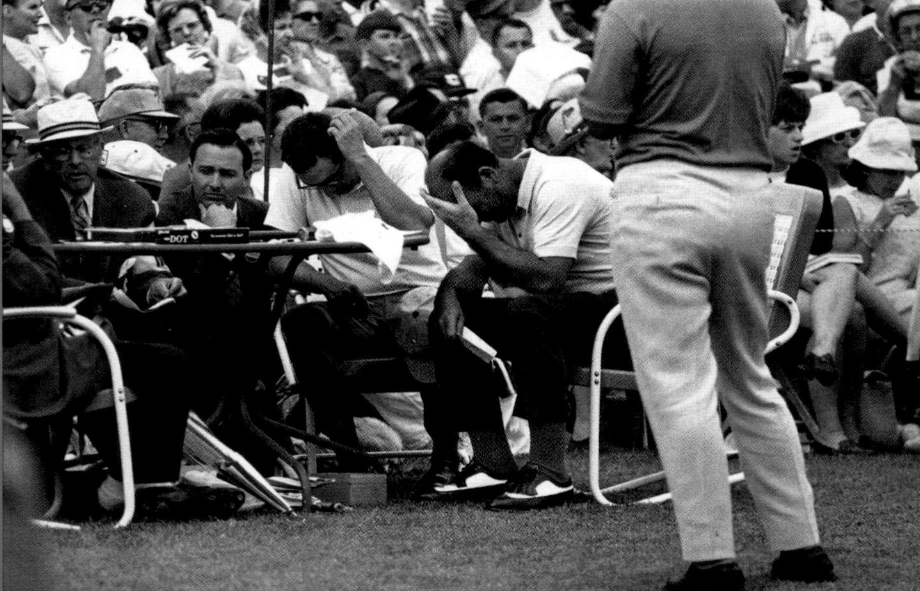

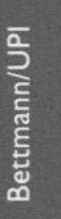

30

27 ***To the swift goes the view: Spectators at the 1965 Masters sprint for prime spots.***

28 ***In the 1960 Open, Tommy Bolt throws club after ball into a Cherry Hills lake.***

29 ***Payne Stewart (foreground), Dave Stockton, and Mark O'Meara (deep in water) take a victory plunge after the American win in the 1991 Ryder Cup.***

30 ***At the 1968 Masters, Roberto De Vicenzo (seated right) takes it hard after having signed an incorrect scorecard, kept by Tommy Aaron (on his right).***

Chronology of the Game

David Barrett

1457
The first written mention of the sport of golf comes in an Act of Parliament in Scotland, which outlaws the game because it interferes with archery practice. The law apparently has little effect.

1744
The Honourable Company of Edinburgh Golfers, the first known golf club, is formed in Edinburgh, Scotland. It also establishes the first official rules.

USGA Collection

The Royal & Ancient clubhouse at St. Andrews

1764
The course in St. Andrews, Scotland, is reduced from twenty-two holes to eighteen, which becomes the standard, as the Royal & Ancient Golf Club of St. Andrews becomes the game's authority.

1786
A golf club is formed in Charleston, South Carolina. Golf is also played in Savannah, Georgia, but the game dies out in these isolated American hamlets after about twenty-five years.

1848
The gutta-percha ball is introduced. Made from the sap of an Asian tree, it is cheaper, more durable, and flies farther than the old feather-stuffed ball, and soon becomes the ball of choice.

1860
The first British Open championship is played at the Prestwick Golf Club in Scotland.

1873
The Royal Montreal Golf Club is organized, the oldest operating golf club in North America.

1887
The first instruction book with photographs—*The Art of Golf*, by Sir Walter Simpson—is published.

1888
The St. Andrew's Golf Club is formed in Yonkers, New York, on November fourteenth. Golf has been played on a scattered basis in the United States for the past decade or so, but St. Andrew's is the first documented club of this era.

1890
The Hotel Champlain in Bluff Point, New York, opens the first American resort course.

1892
Shinnecock Hills Golf Club, established in 1891, becomes the first American course to get a clubhouse. It is designed by famed architect Stanford White. Shinnecock Hills also becomes the first club with a waiting list for membership.

1894
A. G. Spalding sells the first American-made golf club.

In September, William G. Lawrence wins a "national amateur championship" at Newport (Rhode Island) Golf Club. In October, Laurence B. Stoddard wins a "national amateur championship" at St. Andrew's Golf Club. C. B. Macdonald, runner-up in both events, calls for the formation of a body to run a universally recognized national championship.

The Amateur Golf Association of the United States—soon to be called the United States Golf Association—is formed on December 22. Charter members are Newport Golf Club, Shinnecock Hills Golf Club, The Country Club (Brookline, Massachusetts), St. Andrew's Golf Club, and Chicago Golf Club.

Tacoma Golf Club is the first golf course on the west coast.

1895
America's first eighteen-hole

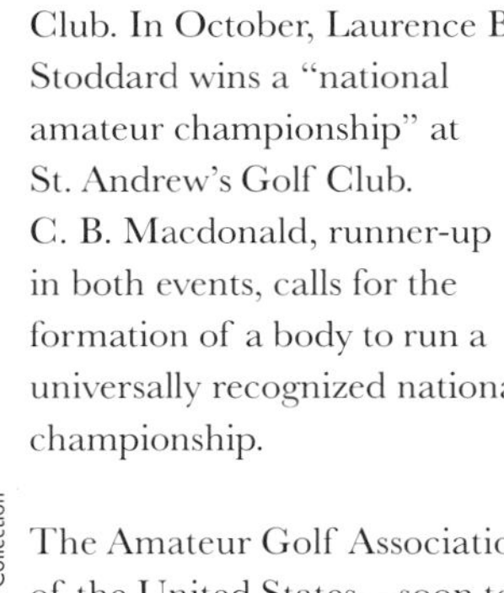
USGA Collection

Charles B. Macdonald

course, Chicago Golf Club, opens.

Charles B. Macdonald wins the first official U.S. Amateur championship at Newport Golf Club. The first U.S. Open is held the next day at the same club, almost as an afterthought to the Amateur. Horace Rawlins wins the $150 first prize over a field of eleven.

The USGA forbids Richard Peters to putt with a pool cue in the U.S. Amateur.

Mrs. Charles S. Brown wins the first U.S. Women's Amateur championship at the Meadow Brook Club in Hempstead, New York.

Golf in America: A Practical Manual, by James Lee, is the first golf book published in the U.S.

Van Cortlandt Park, America's first public course, opens in New York City.

1897
America's first golf magazine, *Golf*, is published.

Yale wins the first collegiate golf championship.

1898
Beatrix Hoyt wins her third straight U.S. Women's Amateur at Ardsley Club in New York. Two years later, she retires at the age of twenty.

Coburn Haskell designs and patents a wound-rubber golf ball, which flies farther than the gutta-percha ball.

The U.S. Open expands to seventy-two holes from thirty-six and is held for the first time at a separate course from the Amateur.

USGA Collection

Van Cortlandt Park Golf Course

Courtesy The Tufts Archives

Harry Vardon's 1900 exhibition tour

The term "birdie" is coined at Atlantic City Country Club in New Jersey when Ab Smith says a fellow member hit a "bird of a shot" and suggests a double payoff for scoring one under par on a hole.

1900

British star Harry Vardon shows Americans a thing or two about how to play the game. In the country for an exhibition tour, he wins the U.S. Open over fellow Englishman J. H. Taylor. The nearest American is ten strokes behind.

Americans Charles Sands and Margaret Abbot win gold medals in golf in the Olympic Games in Paris.

Bettmann/UPI

Walter Travis

Walter J. Travis, who took up golf in 1897 at age thirty-five, wins the U.S. Amateur.

Golf has grown so quickly in America that there are over a thousand courses in the U.S., including one in each of the forty-five states.

1901

Walter Travis wins his second straight U.S. Amateur championship and publishes an instruction book, *Practical Golf.* He's the first to win a major championship playing a Haskell wound-rubber ball.

The pros resist the Haskell ball saying it's hard to control around the greens. Willie Anderson ties Alex Smith with a record-high 331 in the U.S. Open and takes the playoff with an 85. Next year, however, Sandy Herd wins the British Open and Laurence Auchterlonie the U.S. Open with the Haskell, marking the end of the gutta-percha era.

1902

Willie Anderson wins the Western Open with a 299 total, the first time 300 is broken for seventy-two holes in an American event.

Clubmakers in Great Britain begin experimenting with grooved faces in irons. In ten years, smooth-faced irons are on the way out.

1903

Oakmont County Club opens near Pittsburgh, quickly gaining a reputation as one of the nation's toughest tests because of its penal style of architecture.

Pinehurst resort in North Carolina opens its No. 2 course, the seminal work of Donald Ross, who goes on to design hundreds of courses in the United States.

Walter Travis, known as "The Old Man," wins his third U.S. Amateur at age forty-one.

1904

Willie Anderson sets U.S. Open records with a 72 in the final round and a 303 total. Americans claim Australian-born Walter Travis as the first of their own to win the British Amateur. He uses the center-shafted Schenectady putter. In 1910, the R&A bans the center-shafted putter, while the USGA keeps it legal, marking the first time that the USGA diverges from an R&A ruling.

J. H. Taylor sets a British Open record with a 68 in the final round at Royal St. George's, but finishes second to Jack White.

J. H. Oke wins the first Canadian Open.

Courtesy Cambridge Golf Antiquities, Ltd.

Willie Anderson (seated center, with his arm around Alex Smith)

1905

Twenty-seven-year-old Willie Anderson wins his third straight U.S. Open and fourth in five years. It's also his last Open victory; he dies in 1910.

In Great Britain, William Taylor patents a dimple design for golf-ball covers.

Harry Vardon publishes *The Complete Golfer,* which explains, among other things, the overlapping, or Vardon, grip.

Courtesy Ralph W. Miller Golf Library/Museum

Harry Vardon

1906

Three-time U.S. Open runner-up Alex Smith finally wins one, and he's the first to break 300 in an Open. His brother Willie is second. In 1910, Alex wins his second Open by beating his other brother, Macdonald.

1907

Arnaud Massy of France becomes the first foreigner to win the British Open.

Margaret Curtis beats her sister Harriot in an all-in-the-family final of the U.S. Women's Amateur.

1908

Jerry Travers wins his second straight U.S. Amateur.

Three-time U.S. Amateur champion Walter Travis shows he's a jack-of-all-trades by founding *American Golfer* magazine and serving as its first editor. He's also a golf-course designer.

The Mystery of Golf, by Arnold Haultain, is the first instruction book on the mental side of the game.

1909

David Hunter sets a U.S. Open record with a 68 in the first round, but ends up tied for thirty-first.

Robert Gardner becomes the youngest U.S. Amateur champion at age nineteen.

New president William Howard Taft is the first golf-loving occupant of the White House.

The Bettmann Archive

Alex Smith (teeing off)

The USGA rules that caddies, caddiemasters, and greenkeepers past the age of sixteen are considered professionals. The age would be raised to eighteen in 1930, twenty-one in 1945, and the ruling would be rescinded in 1963.

1910

Arthur F. Knight obtains a patent for a seamed, tubular steel golf shaft. Steel shafts, however, are still illegal.

1911

Johnny McDermott signals the end of dominance by Scottish-born professionals in early American golf by becoming the first native to win the U.S. Open. At age nineteen, he's also the youngest-ever winner.

Englishman Harold Hilton is the first player to win the British and U.S. Amateurs in the same year.

The USGA increases yardages for determining par:
Three—up to 225 yards
Four—226 to 425 yards
Five—426 to 600 yards
Six—601 yards and over

1912
John Ball wins his eighth British Amateur championship—still a record number of victories in a major event.

The USGA introduces a handicap limit of six on entrants for the U.S. Amateur.

Bill Anderson Collection

Francis Ouimet at the 1914 U.S. Open

1913
Twenty-year-old American amateur Francis Ouimet stages the game's biggest upset, beating English stars Harry Vardon and Ted Ray in a playoff to win the U.S. Open at The Country Club in Brookline, Massachusetts. The resultant headlines spark a surge of interest in the game in America.

Jerry Travers wins his fourth U.S. Amateur.

The first professional international match is held between a team of four American and four French professionals at La Boulie, in Versailles, France.

1914
Harry Vardon wins his sixth British Open, one more than each of the other two members of the "Great Triumvirate," J. H. Taylor and James Braid.

Walter Hagen, a stylish twenty-one-year-old pro, wins the first of his two U.S. Open titles, leading after every round.

Francis Ouimet becomes the first with career U.S. Open and Amateur titles, beating Jerry Travers in the final of the U.S. Amateur.

1915
Jerry Travers adds the U.S. Open to his four U.S. Amateur crowns, then retires at age twenty-eight.

All British and Canadian championships are suspended because of World War I. They resume in Canada in 1919; in Britain in 1920.

USGA Collection

Alexa Stirling

1916
The amateur run on the U.S. Open continues. Chick Evans is the third amateur to win in four years (shooting a record 286); he's also the first to capture the U.S. Open and Amateur titles in the same year.

Bobby Jones makes his U.S. Amateur debut at age fourteen, reaching the quarterfinals at Merion Cricket Club.

The Professional Golfers' Association of America is formed in January. In October, Jim Barnes wins the first PGA Championship, taking the $500 first prize.

The first miniature golf course opens in Pinehurst, North Carolina.

Francis Ouimet loses his amateur status after opening a sporting goods business.

1917
The USGA championships (U.S. Open, U.S. Amateur, Women's Amateur) and the PGA Championship are suspended in 1917 and 1918 because of World War I.

Fifteen-year-old Bobby Jones wins the Southern Amateur.

Par yardages changed:
Three—up to 250 yards
Four—251 to 445 yards
Five—446 to 600 yards
Six—over 600 yards

1918
George Crump, founder and designer of Pine Valley Golf Club, dies; only fourteen holes of the New Jersey course have been completed. The remaining holes open within a few years.

The USGA restores Francis Ouimet's amateur standing.

Among the fund-raising tours by pro and amateur golfers for the war effort, the Dixie Kids—featuring Atlanta teenagers Bobby Jones and Alexa Stirling—raise $150,000 for the Red Cross.

1919
Pebble Beach Golf Links opens on California's Monterey Peninsula.

USGA Collection

President Harding awards Jim Barnes the trophy at the 1921 U.S. Open.

The first golf book to use high-speed sequence photography—*Picture Analysis of Golf Strokes*, by Jim Barnes—is published.

1920
Fifty-year-old Harry Vardon, playing in his third U.S. Open, plays the last seven holes in even 5s to finish second, one stroke behind his English countryman, forty-three-year-old Ted Ray. Ray becomes the oldest man to win the Open (a record that will stand until 1986).

Alexa Stirling wins her third straight Women's Amateur (1916, 1919, 1920—the tournament wasn't held in 1917 and 1918).

The USGA creates the Green Section for turfgrass research.

The USGA and R&A agree to a standard ball—1.62 inches in diameter and 1.62 ounces.

Pinehurst Country Club opens the first practice range, dubbed "Maniac Hill."

1921
Jim Barnes romps to a nine-stroke win in the U.S. Open, and President Warren Harding, a USGA Executive Committee member, presents the trophy at Columbia Country Club near Washington, D.C.

Jock Hutchison wins the British Open using deep-grooved irons—which will be banned four years later.

1922
A Cinderella story: twenty-year-old Gene Sarazen, a sixth-grade dropout from a working-class family, wins the U.S. Open and PGA Championship.

An admission fee ($1) is charged for the first time at the U.S. Open.

Walter Hagen becomes the first American-born player to win the British Open.

Intended for all interested countries, the first Walker

Courtesy Ralph W. Miller Golf Library/Museum

Gene Sarazen, appearing at a "night golf" range

Cup Match between amateurs from the U.S. and Great Britain (the only taker) is held at National Golf Links of America in Southampton, New York. The U.S. wins.

Public-course golfers get their own tournament—the USGA's Amateur Public Links championship.

Glenna Collett wins the first of six U.S. Women's Amateurs.

Walter Hagen is the first pro to found a golf equipment company under his name.

USGA Collection

A.W. Tillinghast

1923
Winged Foot Golf Club opens, with thirty-six holes designed by A. W. Tillinghast. Designers like Tillinghast, Donald Ross, and Alister Mackenzie make the 1920s the golden age of golf architecture.

After several near misses in the U.S. Open and U.S. Amateur, twenty-one-year-old Bobby Jones claims his first major title by beating Bobby Cruickshank in a playoff for the U.S. Open.

The Texas Open, in its second year, has golf's biggest purse yet—$6,000. Walter Hagen wins. The tournament is part of a growing winter circuit for the pros.

Gene Sarazen beats Walter Hagen in a classic thirty-eight-hole final at the PGA Championship when a tree stops Sarazen's ball from going out of bounds on the deciding hole.

1924
Steel-shafted clubs are permitted in the U.S. by the USGA as of April 11; the R&A continues to ban their use in Great Britain until 1929.

Bobby Jones wins the first of his five U.S. Amateur titles, at Merion Cricket Club in Ardmore, Pennsylvania.

The Bettmann Archive

Gallery at 1924 U.S. Amateur

Walter Hagen's unmatched reign begins in the PGA Championship—he wins the first of four straight titles.

The USGA introduces sectional qualifying rounds for the U.S. Open.

1925
Willie Macfarlane shoots a record 67 in the second round of the U.S. Open and goes on to beat Bobby Jones in a playoff.

The first complete fairway irrigation system is installed at Brook Hollow Country Club in Dallas, Texas.

The Havemeyer Trophy, which goes to the U.S. Amateur champion, is destroyed in a fire at Bobby Jones's home club, East Lake in Atlanta.

1926
Bobby Jones is the first to win the U.S. and British Opens in the same year.

Harry Cooper wins the first Los Angeles Open, which carries a $10,000 purse.

Walter Hagen beats Leo Diegel in the final of the PGA Championship. The night before, when a carousing Hagen is told his opponent had long since gone to bed, he replies, "Yes, but he isn't sleeping."

Walter Hagen wallops Bobby Jones, 12 and 11, in a seventy-two-hole challenge match billed as the "world championship."

Two million Americans are now playing the game.

Jess Sweetser is the first American to win the British Amateur since Walter Travis in 1904—and the first U.S. native ever.

1927
Walter Hagen wins his fourth consecutive PGA Championship. After winning the semifinals when Al Espinosa three-putts the thirty-sixth and thirty-seventh holes, Hagen says, "What are you going to do? You give these boys a chance and they don't take it."

The U.S. Department of Agriculture says it has developed "the perfect putting green grass"—creeping bent.

Bobby Jones wins the British Open and U.S. Amateur, and publishes *Down the Fairway*.

The Bettmann Archive

Celebrating Jess Sweetser's win at the 1926 British Amateur

The U.S. whips Great Britain, 9-1/2 to 2-1/2, in the inaugural Ryder Cup match at Worcester Country Club in Massachusetts.

1928
Cypress Point Golf Club opens in Pebble Beach, California.

Walter Hagen wins the British Open. He would take his final title in the event the following year at Muirfield.

Bobby Jones and Glenna Collett continue to dominate amateur golf. Jones wins the U.S. Amateur final by a 10 and 9 margin, Collett the Women's Amateur, 13 and 12.

1929
Great Britain evens the fledgling Ryder Cup series by winning on its home turf.

Twenty-year-old Horton Smith sweeps out of Missouri to win eight pro tournaments, including four in a row in the spring.

The world's two best women amateurs meet in the British Ladies' Amateur. Great Britain's Joyce Wethered beats America's Glenna Collett, 3 and 1, at the Old Course in St. Andrews, Scotland, claiming her fourth British title.

The U.S. Amateur goes to the west coast for the first time, at Pebble Beach Golf Links. Bobby Jones is a first-round upset victim.

1930
Bobby Jones wins the Grand Slam—the U.S. Open, U.S. Amateur, British Open and British Amateur—then retires at age twenty-eight.

The $25,000 Agua Caliente Open in Tijuana, Mexico, is the richest tournament yet. Gene Sarazen takes the $10,000 first prize.

Courtesy Ralph W. Miller/Golf Library/Museum

Bobby Jones at St. Andrews, 1930

Bettmann/UPI

Gene Sarazen, the center of attention at the 1932 U.S. Open

Glenna Collett wins her third straight U.S. Women's Amateur.

The onset of the Depression brings on a slowdown in golf-course construction which lasts through the end of World War II.

1931

The USGA mandates use of a larger and lighter ball (1.68 inches and 1.55 ounces). This so-called "balloon ball" is very unpopular, and after only one year the USGA increases the allowed weight to 1.62 ounces, keeping the size at 1.68 inches. Meanwhile, the R&A stays with the 1.62-inch, 1.62-ounce ball.

The concave-faced wedge is banned. But Gene Sarazen perfects his design of the sand wedge, with a wide flange, which will remain legal.

Bobby Jones films a series of instructional movies, "How I Play Golf."

Billy Burke is the first to win a U.S. Open using steel shafts. It takes him seventy-two extra holes (two thirty-six-hole playoffs) to beat George Von Elm.

1932

Gene Sarazen wins the U.S. and British Opens, with record scores of 286 and 283, respectively. He finishes the U.S. Open with a record 66.

The first Curtis Cup Match, between women amateurs of the U.S. and Great Britain, is won by the U.S., 5-1/2 to 3-1/2.

USGA Collection

Glenna Collett (on left) congratulates 1932 Women's Amateur champ Virginia Van Wie

1933

Augusta National Golf Club, founded by Bobby Jones, has its grand opening in January.

Johnny Goodman is the fifth—and most recent—amateur to win the U.S. Open.

1934

Horton Smith wins the first Augusta National Invitational. Its name will be changed to The Masters the following year.

Lawson Little wins the U.S. and British Amateurs, the "Little Slam," a feat he will repeat next year.

England's Henry Cotton ties the British Open record with a 67 in the first round and breaks it with a 65 in the second. His victory is the first by a Briton in eleven years.

Virginia Van Wie wins the U.S. Women's Amateur for the third straight year.

Joseph C. Dey, Jr., is appointed executive secretary of the USGA. He will hold the post for thirty-four years.

Helen Hicks is the first woman to turn professional. There are no pro tournaments, but she promotes products for Wilson Sporting Goods Company.

1935

Gene Sarazen strikes the most famous shot in the history of the American game—a double eagle on Augusta National's fifteenth hole, which ties Craig Wood during the final round. Sarazen wins the playoff the next day.

Glenna Collett Vare wins her sixth U.S. Women's Amateur.

1936

Lawson Little turns professional instead of going for a third straight U.S.–British Amateur sweep.

Unheralded Tony Manero closes with a 67 to win the U.S. Open with a record 282.

In winning the U.S. Amateur, Johnny Fischer is the last to capture a national championship using hickory shafts.

1937

Sam Snead bursts onto the pro circuit with five victories but finishes second in his first U.S. Open, a tournament he never wins despite repeated attempts (Ralph Guldahl becomes champion with a record 281.)

AP/Wide World Photos

Sam Snead in 1937

The first Bing Crosby National Pro-Am is held at Rancho Santa Fe in San Diego. It will move to Pebble Beach in 1947.

Byron Nelson wins The Masters, making up six strokes on Ralph Guldahl on the twelfth and thirteenth holes of the final round.

Denny Shute wins his second consecutive PGA Championship.

The U.S. wins the Ryder Cup on British soil for the first time.

1938

A new USGA Rule limits players to fourteen clubs. Some players (e.g., Lawson Little) have been carrying as many as twenty-five; the Rule is designed to restore shot-making skill.

Courtesy The Country Club

Lawson Little and David Goldman in 1934

Sam Snead wins eight tournaments and shatters the earnings record with $19,534.

Ralph Guldahl wins his second consecutive U.S. Open, and third consecutive Western Open. Shortly thereafter, he writes an instructional book and his game disappears.

Patty Berg, twice a runner-up, wins the U.S. Women's Amateur at age twenty.

Ray Ainsley makes the highest score on a hole in U.S. Open history, a nineteen on the sixteenth hole at Cherry Hills. Most of the strokes come as he tries to hit the ball out of a creek.

1939

The Ryder Cup is canceled because of the war in Europe.

Byron Nelson wins the U.S. Open in a playoff over Craig Wood and Denny Shute after Sam Snead blows the tournament by making an eight on the seventy-second hole.

1940
The Walker Cup is canceled because of the war. The British Open and Amateur also are canceled.

Ben Hogan wins his first individual title, then takes the next two events as well. He leads the money list from 1940 to 1942.

USGA Collection

Jimmy Demaret (on left) at the 1957 U.S. Open

Jimmy Demaret, the most colorful golfer of his generation, wins the first of three Masters titles despite Lloyd Mangrum's tournament-record round of 64.

Craig Wood shoots a stunning 264 for seventy-two holes in winning the Metropolitan (NY) Open.

Porky Oliver would have tied for first in the U.S. Open, but he is disqualified from the playoff for starting his last round before he was scheduled to, along with five others, while trying to beat a storm. Lawson Little defeats Gene Sarazen for the title.

Byron Nelson beats Sam Snead, one up, in a match of titans for the PGA Championship.

1941
Craig Wood ends a string of frustrating runner-up finishes in major events by winning both The Masters and the U.S. Open.

The USGA develops a machine for testing golf-ball velocity at impact. Plans for implementing a new rule limiting initial velocity are put on hold until after the war.

1942
A Rule change authorizes players to stop play on their own initiative if they consider themselves endangered by lightning.

The USGA cancels all its championships for the duration of the war. The PGA of America continues its Tour schedule, though it is an abbreviated one.

The U.S. government halts the manufacturing of golf equipment.

Sam Snead wins the PGA Championship. He had been granted a delay of several days before induction into the Navy so he could play in the event.

Byron Nelson beats Ben Hogan in a playoff for The Masters.

Ben Hogan wins the Hale America National Open, a fund-raising event which takes the place of the U.S. Open during the war years.

1943
The war takes a heavy toll on competitive golf. The PGA Tour is reduced to only three tournaments. There is no PGA Championship.

The Masters is canceled for the duration of the war.

1944
The PGA Tour is back up to twenty-two tournaments, though many players are in military service. The PGA Championship returns, with Bob Hamilton upsetting heavily favored Byron Nelson in the final.

The Tam O'Shanter Open offers a record purse of $42,000 and is won by Byron Nelson, who is exempt from military service because of a blood disorder.

1945
Byron Nelson wins a record eleven straight tournaments from March through August, and eighteen during the year. While fields aren't back at full strength, Sam Snead and Ben Hogan each are on hand for part of the year.

Ben Hogan sets a seventy-two-hole scoring record with 261; two weeks later, Byron Nelson breaks it with 259.

1946
Ben Hogan wins thirteen PGA Tour events, including the PGA Championship, but loses The Masters and the U.S. Open by one stroke.

Sam Snead wins the British Open at the Old Course in St. Andrews, Scotland. On passing the course on a train on his way to the tournament, Snead declares, "That looks like an old, abandoned golf course," a remark much reported in the British press.

The first U.S. Women's Open is held, and the only one ever at match play. Patty Berg wins.

Byron Nelson retires at age thirty-four after winning six tournaments during the year.

Bettmann/UPI

Byron Nelson and his caddie Donnie Fox

1947
The USGA revises and simplifies the *Rules of Golf*, going from sixty-one Rules to twenty-one. The R&A doesn't go along, however.

South African Bobby Locke storms onto the PGA Tour with six victories.

The U.S. Open is first televised—but only locally, on KSD-TV in St. Louis.

Babe Didrikson Zaharias is the first American to win the Ladies' British Open Amateur. She turns pro later in the year.

Golf World magazine begins publishing.

1948
The first U.S. Junior Amateur is played, with Dean Lind beating Ken Venturi in the final match.

Bobby Locke wins the Chicago Victory National Championship by a PGA Tour record sixteen strokes.

Ben Hogan wins his first of four U.S. Opens with a record score of 276. He also wins the PGA Championship.

Golf Journal magazine—originally *USGA Journal Combining Timely Turf Topics*—appears.

African-American pros Ted Rhodes and Bill Spiller finish in the top twenty-five at the Los Angeles Open, one of the few tournaments open to African-Americans. They remain excluded from most PGA Tour events under a rule that leaves the decision up to tournament sponsors.

Bettmann/UPI

Bill Spiller at the Los Angeles Open

1949
Sam Snead, recovering from a bout with the putting yips, wins The Masters by finishing 67-67. Later, he adds the PGA Championship.

Marlene Bauer, age fifteen, wins the first U.S. Girls' Junior championship, and turns pro later in the year.

AP/Wide World Photos

Craig Wood at the 1941 Masters

Louise Suggs wins the U.S. Women's Open by fourteen strokes.

Harry Bradshaw hits a shot from inside a broken beer bottle during the final round of the British Open instead of waiting for a ruling (relief would have been granted). He ties Bobby Locke, and loses a playoff.

1950
Ben Hogan returns to the Tour a year after nearly being killed in an automobile accident—and wins the U.S. Open at Merion.

Lee Mackey is the first to shoot a 64 in the U.S. Open. The next day, he shoots 81.

The Ladies Professional Golf Association, under dynamic tournament manager Fred Corcoran, replaces the struggling Women's Professional Golf Association.

Jimmy Demaret wins his third Masters.

Babe Zaharias wins the U.S. Women's Open by nine strokes.

Sam Snead wins eleven events on the PGA Tour.

1951
The USGA and R&A hold a joint conference and agree on a uniform Rules of Golf worldwide, effective the following year. The only remaining difference is the size of the ball (the R&A permits a diameter of 1.62 inches compared with the USGA's 1.68 inches). The stymie is abolished, center-shafted putters are legalized (in Britain, center-shafted putters had been illegal since shortly after Travis's 1904 British Amateur victory), and the out-of-bounds penalty made stroke and distance.

Ben Hogan wins The Masters and a second consecutive U.S. Open. The latter victory comes at Oakland Hills, deemed a "monster" after its redesign by Robert Trent Jones in 1950.

Golf Digest magazine begins publishing.

Al Brosch shoots a PGA Tour record 60 during the Texas Open.

1952
Dwight David Eisenhower is elected U.S. President; during his eight years in office, his cottage at Augusta National becomes the "Little White House."

Jack Burke, Jr., wins four consecutive events on the PGA Tour, second in history to Byron Nelson's eleven straight.

Patty Berg shoots an LPGA record 64 in the Richmond Open.

Julius Boros captures the U.S. Open. He also wins the biggest first-place prize, $25,000, at the World Championship.

1953
Ben Hogan takes the three majors he enters—The Masters, U.S. Open, and British Open. It is his fourth U.S. Open title.

The first nationally televised tournament, the World Championship, ends with a moment of high drama when Lew Worsham holes out from 104 yards to eagle the final hole and wins by one.

Courtesy Winged Foot Golf Club

Tommy Armour

Tommy Armour's popular instruction book, *How to Play Your Best Golf All the Time*, is published.

1954
The U.S. Open is televised nationally for the first time. Also new—the holes are roped for gallery control.

USGA Collection

Babe Zaharias, 1954 U.S. Women's Open champion

Babe Zaharias wins the U.S. Women's Open by twelve strokes a year after undergoing cancer surgery.

Amateur Gene Littler wins the San Diego Open on the PGA Tour.

Chandler Harper shoots 63s in each of the last three rounds to win the Texas Open, a 54-hole scoring record which still stands.

Sam Snead beats Ben Hogan in a playoff to win The Masters after amateur Billy Joe Patton falters on the back nine of regulation.

The World Championship has the first $100,000 purse, with $50,000 going to the winner—five times more than the next biggest first prize. Bob Toski earns the windfall.

1955
Mike Souchak wins the Texas Open with a seventy-two-hole total of 257—a PGA Tour record that still stands.

Unheralded Jack Fleck stuns Ben Hogan with his U.S. Open playoff win.

Arnold Palmer scores his first professional victory in the Canadian Open.

Life magazine pays Ben Hogan $20,000 for a cover story revealing the "secret" he discovered nine years earlier which rid him of a hook.

1956
Jack Burke, Jr., makes up an eight-stroke deficit on amateur Ken Venturi to win The Masters. Burke also takes the PGA Championship.

Australian Peter Thomson wins his third straight British Open.

Cary Middlecoff captures his second U.S. Open title.

Yardages for guidance in computing par are increased to current levels:
Three—up to 250 yards
Four—251 to 470 yards
Five—471 and over

1957
Harvie Ward, the U.S. Amateur champion, is declared ineligible as an amateur for accepting expenses to golf events. (He will be reinstated in 1958.)

Jackie Pung finishes as the apparent winner of the U.S. Women's Open, but is disqualified for signing an incorrect scorecard. Betsy Rawls takes the title.

Bettmann/UPI

Betsy Rawls, surprised U.S. Open winner

Bobby Locke wins his fourth British Open with a record-tying 279.

Great Britain triumphs in the Ryder Cup for the first time since 1933.

Ben Hogan publishes an instruction classic: *Five Lessons: The Modern Fundamentals of Golf.*

Archive Photos

New York City ticker-tape parade for Ben Hogan after his 1953 British Open win.

1958
PGA Tour prize money surpasses $1 million.

New USGA system provides just one handicap for golfers, not "current" and "basic."

Arnold Palmer wins the first of his four Masters titles.

At age twenty-three, Mickey Wright sweeps the U.S. Women's Open and LPGA Championship.

The PGA Championship is switched from match play to stroke play; Dow Finsterwald claims the title.

The rich World Championship of Golf drops off the PGA Tour schedule after tournament sponsor George S. May feuds with the pros.

USGA and R&A organize the World Amateur Golf Council, and hold the first World Amateur Team Championship at the Old Course, St. Andrews, Scotland.

1959
Mickey Wright wins her second consecutive U.S. Women's Open.

Bill Wright becomes the first African-American player to take a national championship, claiming the U.S. Amateur Public Links.

Nineteen-year-old Jack Nicklaus finishes first in the U.S. Amateur.

Betsy Rawls wins ten LPGA tournaments.

Golf magazine begins publishing.

1960
Arnold Palmer, golf's most popular player, has his greatest year. He wins The Masters with birdies on the last two holes, the U.S. Open with a final-round 65, finishes second in the British Open, and wins eight PGA Tour events.

Rules regarding the putting green are liberalized to permit cleaning the ball and repairing ballmarks.

Betsy Rawls wins her fourth U.S. Women's Open.

1961
Mickey Wright wins three majors—the U.S. Women's Open, LPGA Championship, and the Titleholders—and ten events in all.

The PGA of America drops the Caucasian clause from its constitution, allowing African-Americans to become members. Most tournaments have opened the door to African-Americans.

Arnold Palmer wins the British Open; his appearances in the event starting in 1960 convince more American players to make the trip.

Bettmann/UPI

Arnold Palmer with sports writers in 1962

Jerry Barber sinks monster putts of forty and sixty feet on the last two holes to tie Don January for the PGA Championship; Barber then wins the eighteen-hole playoff by a stroke.

Anne Quast Decker wins the U.S. Women's Amateur by a record 14 and 13 margin over Phyllis Preuss.

There are now 5 million golfers in the U.S., according to the National Golf Foundation.

1962
Rookie pro Jack Nicklaus beats hometown favorite Arnold Palmer to win the U.S. Open in a playoff at Oakmont Country Club near Pittsburgh.

Arnold Palmer wins The Masters, British Open, and seven PGA Tour events.

Mickey Wright wins ten tournaments for the second consecutive year.

Water hazards are first marked with painted lines on the ground at the U.S. Open.

1963
Arnold Palmer is the first player to surpass $100,000 in earnings in a single year.

Jack Nicklaus wins The Masters and PGA Championship.

At the age of twenty years, six months, Ray Floyd is the youngest player to win a PGA Tour event (the St. Petersburg Open) since 1928.

New Zealand's Bob Charles becomes the only left-hander to win one of the four major championships, claiming the British Open.

Mickey Wright wins thirteen events on the LPGA Tour.

Clubmakers are experimenting with the casting method for making irons, enabling them to create a larger "sweet spot" than forged blades offer.

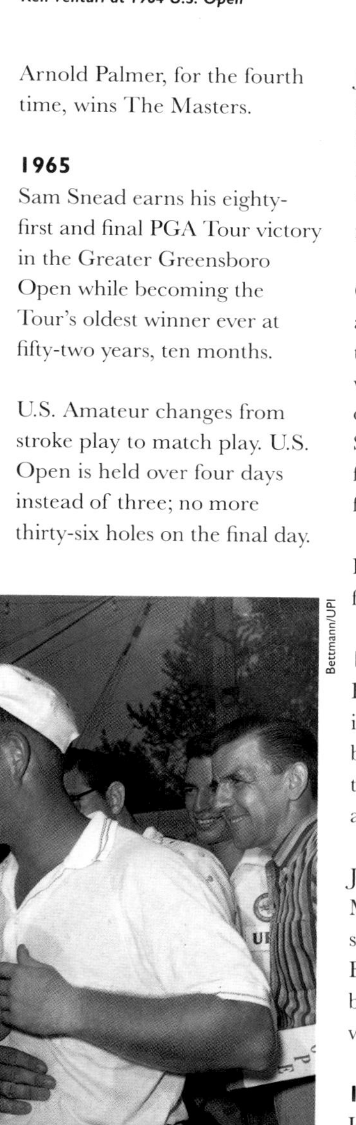
James Drake

Ken Venturi at 1964 U.S. Open

1964
Ken Venturi wins the U.S. Open despite suffering from heat prostration during a thirty-six-hole final day at Congressional Country Club outside Washington, D.C.

Mickey Wright wins her fourth U.S. Women's Open. She captures eleven tournaments during the year and sets an LPGA eighteen-hole record with a 62.

Bobby Nichols wins the PGA Championship with a seventy-two-hole total of 271, a record that still stands.

Arnold Palmer, for the fourth time, wins The Masters.

1965
Sam Snead earns his eighty-first and final PGA Tour victory in the Greater Greensboro Open while becoming the Tour's oldest winner ever at fifty-two years, ten months.

U.S. Amateur changes from stroke play to match play. U.S. Open is held over four days instead of three; no more thirty-six holes on the final day.

Jack Nicklaus wins The Masters by nine strokes with a record 271 total. Tournament host Bobby Jones says Nicklaus "plays a game with which I am not familiar."

Gary Player joins Ben Hogan and Gene Sarazen to become the third player in history to win all four majors when he captures the U.S. Open. The South African is the first foreign winner of the Open in forty-five years.

Peter Thomson triumphs in his fifth British Open.

Bettmann/UPI

Arnold Palmer and Jack Nicklaus at the 1962 U.S. Open

1966
Billy Casper wins the U.S. Open in a playoff after Arnold Palmer blows a seven-stroke lead over the last nine holes of regulation at Olympic Club in California.

Jack Nicklaus takes his third Masters in four years and second in a row. He also is the British Open champion, becoming the fourth player to win all four major events.

1967
Jack Nicklaus takes the U.S. Open with a record total of 275 at Baltusrol in New Jersey.

Bettmann/UPI

1968 U.S. Open winner Lee Trevino and runner-up Jack Nicklaus

Catherine Lacoste of France becomes the only amateur to win the U.S. Women's Open.

Forty-five-year-old Charlie Sifford becomes the first African-American player to win a PGA Tour event, capturing the Greater Hartford Open.

1968

Croquet-style putting, recently employed by Sam Snead, is ruled illegal by the USGA.

Tour players threaten to break away from the PGA and form their own organization. The dispute is settled when the Tournament Players Division is created within the PGA.

Roberto de Vicenzo loses The Masters when he signs an incorrect scorecard for one stroke higher than he actually shot. He would have been in an eighteen-hole playoff with Bob Goalby, who is declared the winner.

Lee Trevino is the first player to break 70 for all four rounds in a U.S. Open, winning with a record-tying 275 total.

Forty-eight-year-old Julius Boros is the oldest player to claim a major title, winning the PGA Championship.

JoAnne Gunderson Carner wins her fifth U.S. Women's Amateur.

Arnold Palmer becomes the first player to top $1 million in career earnings.

USGA Collection

Billy Casper

Billy Casper is the first player to surpass $200,000 in earnings in one year.

Kathy Whitworth and Carol Mann each win ten tournaments on the LPGA Tour.

1969

JoAnne Carner is the last amateur to win an LPGA Tour event, the Burdine's Invitational.

Tony Jacklin is the first homebred player to win the British Open in eighteen years.

Larry Ziegler finishes first in the Michigan Golf Classic only to discover the sponsors don't have the money for the purse. The PGA is able to pay only half the purse.

Harbour Town Golf Links, designed by Pete Dye with assistance from Jack Nicklaus, opens on Hilton Head Island, South Carolina, and the first Heritage Classic is played there.

1970

Mickey Wright retires from full-time competition at age thirty-four, while JoAnne Carner turns pro at age thirty after an outstanding amateur career.

England's Tony Jacklin wins the U.S. Open; runner-up Dave Hill grabs headlines by ripping the design of Hazeltine National Golf Club.

Jack Nicklaus wins the British Open in a playoff after Doug Sanders misses a three-foot putt for the title in regulation.

Lanny Wadkins beats Tom Kite by one stroke to win the U.S. Amateur.

1971

Hollis Stacy becomes the only player to win three U.S. Girls' Junior titles.

Lee Trevino sizzles with U.S., British, and Canadian Open victories in a four-week stretch.

Astronaut Alan Shepard takes the game to new frontiers by hitting a six-iron shot during a walk on the moon.

With his PGA Championship, Jack Nicklaus becomes the first player to win all the majors twice.

The number of golfers in the U.S. has doubled in the last ten years—there are now 10 million.

1972

Jack Nicklaus wins The Masters and U.S. Open, then is thwarted in his bid for the Grand Slam by Lee Trevino in the British Open.

The Colgate-Dinah Shore Winners Circle debuts on the LPGA Tour, offering the first six-figure purse in women's golf—$110,000.

Spalding introduces the two-piece Top-Flite ball, constructed with a solid core inside a durable synthetic cover.

Title IX legislation is passed by Congress, forcing colleges to provide more opportunities for female athletes. The expansion of women's college golf increases the talent pool of the LPGA Tour.

Carolyn Cudone wins her fifth straight U.S. Senior Women's Amateur, a record for any USGA event.

1973

Mickey Wright takes the Colgate-Dinah Shore Winners Circle, the last of her eighty-two LPGA Tour victories.

Johnny Miller becomes the U.S. Open champion, firing a record 63 in the final round at Oakmont.

Tom Weiskopf takes five tournaments, including the British Open, in a two-month stretch.

Gene Sarazen, age seventy-one, scores an ace during the British Open at Troon.

USGA Collection

Hollis Stacy

Ben Crenshaw bursts onto the PGA Tour by winning his first event as a member, the San Antonio Texas Open.

The U.S. Amateur returns to match play; the winner is Craig Stadler.

Kathy Whitworth is the LPGA Player of the Year for the seventh time in eight years.

The graphite shaft is introduced, promising greater distance. Its popularity will wane until technology and improvements return it to favor in the 1980s.

AP/Wide World Photos

Kathy Whitworth wins the 1968 Canyon Ladies Golf Classic in Palm Springs

Ken Regan/Camera 5

Johnny Miller

1974
Johnny Miller wins eight PGA Tour events.

Deane Beman becomes Commissioner of the PGA Tour.

The Tournament Players Championship makes its debut.

The Muirfield Village Golf Club, designed by Jack Nicklaus and Desmond Muirhead, opens near Nicklaus's hometown of Columbus, Ohio.

Sandra Haynie sweeps the U.S. Women's Open and LPGA Championship.

The World Golf Hall of Fame opens in Pinehurst, North Carolina.

Jack Nicklaus presents instruction advice in his book *Golf My Way*.

1975
Jack Nicklaus wins his fifth Masters in a classic battle with Tom Weiskopf and Johnny Miller. Nicklaus also takes his fourth PGA Championship.

Lee Elder becomes the first African-American to play in The Masters.

Nineteen-year-old Amy Alcott wins in just her third LPGA Tour event.

1976
Ray Floyd wins The Masters with a record-tying 271 total.

Judy Rankin, with $150,734 in earnings, becomes the first LPGA Tour player to earn more than $100,000 in a season.

The USGA adopts the Overall Distance Standard for golf balls, limiting them to 280 yards under standard test conditions.

Jack Nicklaus leads the PGA Tour in earnings for an eighth and final time.

1977
Al Geiberger is the first PGA Tour player to break 60, shooting a 59 in the Danny Thomas Memphis Classic.

Tom Watson hits the big time, outdueling Jack Nicklaus in both The Masters and the British Open. Watson's 268 sets a British Open record.

The U.S. Open is the first American golf event to provide television coverage of all eighteen holes.

A major championship is decided by sudden death for the first time when Lanny Wadkins beats Gene Littler in the PGA Championship at Pebble Beach.

1978
Nancy Lopez gives the LPGA Tour a boost by winning five tournaments in a row, and nine in all, during her first full season.

PGA Tour purses top $10 million.

Gary Player takes his third Masters by shooting a 64 in the final round, then wins the next two events as well.

Jack Nicklaus's third British Open title gives him at least three wins in all four majors.

The Legends of Golf debuts, an event which will lead to the birth of the Senior Tour.

1979
TaylorMade introduces its first metal wood. In the next decade, metal woods will become predominant.

The USGA plants a tree overnight at the Inverness Club to block a shortcut taken by several players in the first round of the U.S. Open.

Sixty-seven-year-old Sam Snead shoots a 66 during the Quad Cities Open.

Phil Sheldon

Ben Crenshaw

Twenty-two-year-old Seve Ballesteros wins the British Open despite hitting the ball all over Royal Lytham & St. Annes.

1980
Jack Nicklaus captures the U.S. Open (his fourth) and PGA Championship (his fifth) at age 40. He shoots a U.S. Open record 272 in the Open at Baltusrol and ties the eighteen-hole record with a 63.

The USGA adds the U.S. Senior Open to its list of championships.

Tom Watson leads the PGA Tour money list for an unprecedented fourth straight year. He wins six U.S. events plus the British Open.

Tom Weiskopf makes a thirteen on the par-three twelfth hole at Augusta National during The Masters, hitting five balls in the water.

The Tournament Players Club at Sawgrass, designed by Pete Dye, opens in Jacksonville, Florida. It's the first "stadium course," with mounds designed for spectator viewing, and the first course of the PGA Tour's TPC network.

The USGA introduces the Symmetry Standard to the *Rules of Golf*, eliminating balls that correct themselves in flight.

1981
Kathy Whitworth is the first woman player to top $1 million in career earnings.

The USGA adds the U.S. Mid-Amateur championship for players twenty-five and older, an event in which career amateurs won't have to face college golfers, who often dominate the U.S. Amateur.

Tom Kite finishes in the top ten in twenty-one of twenty-six tournaments and leads the PGA Tour money list despite winning only once.

1982
Tom Watson takes his only U.S. Open, chipping in on the seventy-first hole to beat Jack Nicklaus at Pebble Beach.

Juli Inkster takes her third straight U.S. Women's Amateur, the first to accomplish that feat in forty-eight years.

USGA Collection

Sandra Haynie wins the 1974 U.S. Women's Open

Jacqueline Duvoisin/Sports Illustrated

Greg Norman at the 1986 British Open

In the Hawaiian Open, Wayne Levi becomes the first pro to win using an orange ball. He's almost the last (Jerry Pate is the only other one to do it), as orange balls are a short-lived fad.

Kathy Whitworth breaks Mickey Wright's record for career LPGA victories by winning her eighty-third event. She will later take five more.

Jan Stephenson creates controversy with a sexy pose in *Fairway*, the LPGA Tour's official magazine. She also wins the LPGA Championship, and the next year, the U.S. Women's Open.

1983
For the fifth time, Tom Watson is British Open champion.

Andy Bean is penalized two strokes during the third round of the Canadian Open for tapping his ball into the hole with the handle of his putter. The next day, he finishes two strokes out of a playoff.

1984
Golf instruction videotapes begin to hit the market.

Hollis Stacy takes her third U.S. Women's Open to go with her three U.S. Girls' Junior titles.

Forty-four-year-old Lee Trevino is the PGA titleholder, giving him two U.S. Opens, British Opens, and PGAs.

1985
USGA introduces the Slope System to adjust handicaps according to the difficulty of the course being played.

Europe beats the U.S. in the Ryder Cup for the first time since 1957 (the Great Britain and Ireland team was expanded to include all of Europe in 1979). Two years later, the team wins for the first time on U.S. soil.

T.C. Chen blows a four-stroke lead in the U.S. Open—and eventually the championship—by double-hitting a chip shot and making a quadruple bogey on the fifth hole.

1986
Jack Nicklaus, at age forty-six, wins his sixth Masters and eighteenth major professional title.

Nick Price breaks the eighteen-hole record in The Masters with a 63.

Ray Floyd, forty-three, finishes first in the U.S. Open.

Bob Tway holes out from a greenside bunker on the seventy-second hole to break a tie and beat Greg Norman in the PGA Championship.

Pat Bradley wins three LPGA majors—the Nabisco Dinah Shore, LPGA Championship, and du Maurier Classic.

The Panasonic Las Vegas Invitational is the first PGA Tour event with a $1 million purse (actually, $1,150,000).

Total prize money on the LPGA Tour hits $10 million.

The Stadium Course at PGA West in La Quinta, California, designed by Pete Dye, opens. With water galore, deep bunkers, and extreme length (even the pros don't play the back tees), it is billed as the hardest course in the world.

Greg Norman wins nine events worldwide (two in the U.S., three in Europe, and four in Australia).

There are now 20 million golfers in the U.S., and 12,384 courses.

1987
Larry Mize beats Greg Norman in a sudden-death playoff at The Masters by holing a hundred-foot pitch on the second extra hole.

Judy Bell becomes the first woman elected to the USGA Executive Committee.

The PGA Tour tops $30 million in prize money; the new season-ending Nabisco Championship is the first $2 million event.

Don Pooley scores a $1 million ace during the Bay Hill Classic (half for himself, half for charity). Lee Trevino's ace in the Skins Game earns him $175,000—for winning the hole, not as a hole-in-one prize.

Jan Stephenson, tied for the lead after fifty-four holes of the S&H Golf Classic, is in an auto accident. Injuries keep her from playing the final round.

Nick Faldo pars all eighteen holes of the final round in the British Open to win his first major.

Craig Stadler is disqualified from the Shearson Lehman Brothers Andy Williams Open for kneeling on a towel to play

Larry Petrillo

Ray Floyd (right), a champion for more than a quarter of a century, and Payne Stewart at the 1986 U.S. Open

a shot, then signing a scorecard that did not record a two-stroke penalty for his unknowing violation of a Rule that prohibits "building a stance." It costs him second place.

1988

Mary Bea Porter interrupts her qualifying round for the LPGA's Standard Register Classic to resuscitate a boy who had fallen into a nearby swimming pool.

Seve Ballesteros wins his third British Open—one of seven victories during the year in seven different countries.

Curtis Strange becomes the first player to collect $1 million in season earnings on the PGA Tour.

The groove wars begin. The USGA rules that Ping Eye2 irons don't conform to the Rules because the grooves are too close together. Karsten Manufacturing, maker of Pings, files suit. A settlement will be reached in 1990 under which new Pings are modified to conform and existing Pings are deemed acceptable.

1989

PGA Tour purses pass $40 million.

The PGA Tour announces it will ban square-groove irons next year, but Karsten Manufacturing wins a court injunction against the move. Four years later, in an out-of-court settlement, the Tour reverses itself and permits square grooves.

John Iacono/Sports Illustrated

Fred Couples at the 1992 Masters

Curtis Strange wins his second consecutive U.S. Open, the first to do so since Ben Hogan (1950 and 1951).

1990

After a controversy at PGA Championship site Shoal Creek Country Club in Birmingham, Alabama, the PGA of America and PGA Tours announce they will not play tournaments at clubs that have no African-American or women members.

Robert Gamez beats Greg Norman in the Nestle Invitational by holing a seven-iron from 176 yards on the seventy-second hole.

Hale Irwin, forty-five, becomes the oldest U.S. Open winner. He's the first to take a U.S. Open in sudden death, after he ties Mike Donald in an eighteen-hole playoff.

Nick Faldo becomes the first player since Jack Nicklaus (1965 and 1966) to capture a second consecutive Masters. He also wins the British Open.

Phil Mickelson sweeps the U.S. Amateur and NCAA Championship, a feat not accomplished since Jack Nicklaus in 1961.

Lee Trevino takes seven events and collects more than $1 million in his first year on the Senior PGA Tour.

The R&A adopts the American-sized ball (1.68 inches) as standard all over the world.

1991

Long-hitting rookie John Daly overpowers the field in the PGA Championship; he made the field as an alternate.

Robert Walker

USGA Executive Committee members John Merchant (left) and David Boyd

Amateur Phil Mickelson wins the PGA Tour's Northern Telecom Open at age twenty.

Chip Beck shoots a 59 during the Las Vegas Invitational to tie Al Geiberger's PGA Tour record.

Oversized metal woods hit the market, led by Callaway's Big Bertha.

1992

Fred Couples's victory at The Masters puts him over $1 million in earnings in the second week of April.

The PGA Tour tops $50 million in purses; the LPGA and Senior Tours both go over $20 million.

Ray Floyd, forty-nine, wins the Doral Ryder Open twenty-nine years after his first PGA Tour victory. Later in the year, he wins on the Senior Tour.

Betsy King wins the LPGA Championship by eleven strokes with a Tour seventy-two-hole record of 267.

John F. Merchant, a Connecticut attorney, is the first African-American elected to the USGA Executive Committee.

Nick Faldo caps his third British Open.

1993

Bernhard Langer wins his second Masters championship; Greg Norman his second British Open. Norman's 267 total sets a British Open record.

For the third straight time, Tiger Woods is the U.S. Junior Amateur winner. No other player has repeated in the event.

Sarah LeBrun Ingram becomes the first player to take the U.S. Women's Mid-Amateur championship twice. The event began in 1987.

Michael C. Cohen

Sarah LeBrun Ingram

Robert Walker

Phil Mickelson surrounded by fans

Index

Numbers in italic type refer to pages on which photographs appear.

Andy Levin

1993 U.S. Open, Springfield, New Jersey: A church shows its spirit.

USGA Executive Committee
Reg Murphy, Judy Bell, D. Ronald Daniel, F. Morgan Taylor, Jr.,
Gerald A. Stahl, Richard Bennett, David E. Boyd, Thomas W. Chisholm,
James A. Curtis, Trey Holland, Peter W. James, Reed K. Mackenzie,
John F. Merchant, Fred S. Ridley, Richard C. Stroud, Carol Semple Thompson
Leroy Richie, General Counsel; David B. Fay, Executive Director

Project Staff
Editors/Producers: Amy Janello and Brennon Jones, Jones & Janello
Executive Editor for the USGA: Pat Ryan
Publishing Counsel: E. Gabriel Perle
Design: Thomas K. Walker, Graf/x, Sherri Whitmarsh (assistant)
Text Editors: Jon Swan, Leslie Ware
Contributing Editor: Leo Levine
Editorial Researchers: Margaret Morey (chief),
Chiara Peacock, Ari Surdoval, Hunki Yun

USGA Advisors
Mark Carlson, David Earl, John Matheny, Robert Sommers, Don Spencer